Position To Receive

Position To Receive

Michael Matthews

Dominion
Global
Publishing

Position To Receive by Michael Matthews
Published by Dominion Global Publishing
P.O. Box 630372
Houston, Texas 77263
www.positiontoreceive.com
Email: info@positiontoreceive.com

Copyright © 2007 by Michael Matthews
All rights reserved
Library of Congress Control Number:
2006906146
International Standard Book Number:
ISBN (10-digit) 0-9787492-1-9 - Paperback Edition
ISBN (13-digit) 978-0-9787492-1-7 - Paperback Edition
Suggested List Price: $19.95

Book Order Information Contact: Bookworld Companies
1941 Whitfield Park Loop Sarasota, FL 34243 800.444.2524 www.bookworld.com

Book cover design by: D Suave Productions
Book cover concept by: Michael Matthews

Printed in the United States Of America

Publisher's Cataloging-In-Publication Data
(Prepared by The Donohue Group, Inc.)

Matthews, Michael, 1974-
    Position to receive / Michael Matthews.

      p. ; cm.

    ISBN-13: 978-0-9787492-1-7 (pbk.)
    ISBN-10: 0-9787492-1-9 (pbk.)

1. Wealth--Religious aspects--Christianity. 2. Success--Religious aspects--Christianity. 3. Finance, Personal--Religious aspects--Christianity. 4. Conduct of life. I. Title.

BR115.W4 M38 2007
241/.68   2006906146

DEDICATION

This book is dedicated to my beloved wife, Saidia; whom has stood by me unconditionally since day one. You give so much of yourself to me, I couldn't ask for a better helpmate. Your encouragement, motivation and believing in my vision has made this book a reality. You are my true treasure for I appreciate you, value you and love you so very much!

ACKNOWLEDGEMENTS

Position To Receive was inspired by four great men whom have either been a role-model, father-figure, business partner, mentor, advisor, friend or combination:

Dr. Ed Montgomery, my pastor, words can not express my gratitude for your life. I honor you as a businessman and as my spiritual father. God has truly used you in my life. You have imparted into my spirit things that have literally changed my life and changed the world around me. Position To Receive was birth through your ministry and I plan to use it to share with the world, what you have shared with me. May God continue to use you like never before! I love you and I thank you;

Tom McGee, my mentor and business partner, who would have thought nearly 15 years ago, I had the privilege to meet such a wise man. You saw so much of yourself in me and you choose to pour out your knowledge and wisdom into my life. Not only with the business of music but with fatherly advice and true mentorship. You've made so much of your life transparent to me, which has literally kept me from making so many mistakes. I thank God for your life and look forward to many more years of true friendship;

Charles Key, you don't know how much of an impact you have on my life. You allowed me to see how someone my age can achieve anything we set our minds to do. You've been such a strong inspiration to me! I truly believe you are an angel sent from God into my life. I can never thank you enough for the doors you have opened and the opportunities you have shared. You are a true blessing;

Curtis Matthews, my brother whom I love so very much, you sowed into the vision from the very beginning! I don't know where I would be if you had not believed. You choose to give of yourself so I might have, for that I can never repay you. God used you to open the initial door, which has now allowed me to walk into my destiny!

SPECIAL THANKS

To my mother, Joan whom has always believed in me, supported me and showed me what its like to be a survivor! I thank you for giving me life and raising me up to be all I can be. I love you so very much!

Abundant Life Cathedral Family... to all my brothers and sisters in Christ who has supported me, encouraged me, prayed for me and my family, you know who you are! Let's continue to spread this gospel, for He Must Reign Until...

Brad Herndon & Gina Torres, two awesome people who have opened doors for me and even a few windows too! You have always gone above and beyond the call of duty for me in the financial world. I thank you so much for believing in me and supporting this vision. I truly value our relationship and I promise I won't let you down.

Becky Schall of Bookworld Companies, Thank you so much for believing and allowing God to use you that day. You are a true testimony as to what this book is all about. Thanks for helping to make my vision a reality!

To all the individuals whom sowed time, money, knowledge and wisdom into my life since the beginning as there are too many to name... you know who you are. I thank you for sharing and planting the many seeds that has enriched my life forever!

EXTRA SPECIAL THANKS

To Ron, Will, John, Edna, Rosie, Julie, Gay, Becky, Kim and the entire Bookworld Companies staff, thank you so much for all your hard work and time you have put into helping make this release a success. The Bookworld family has been a true blessing to work with, we couldn't ask for a better book distributor!

To my extended family Shawn, Denise, Geraldine, Cheryl, Cindy, Stephanie, Mark, Bryce, Narda, Jonathan, Carl and Betty thanks for all your encouragement and endless support!

To Pastors Dr. Myles Munroe, Bishop Eddie Long, Joel Osteen, Dr. Creflo Dollar, Bishop T.D. Jakes, Dr. Frederick K.C. Price, Tim Storey and many others, your ministries have been a blessing to my life and an inspiration to this book. I thank you and may God continue to use you.

To my many wonderful clients and partners over the years I thank you so much for believing in me and supporting my vision. Without you Dominion Marketing & MJM Management would not exist! Roy Jones Jr. & BodyHead Entertainment; Imani Crosby, TMG Entertainment, Lo End Records, Cool Million Records, B.I.T.T.A. Records, Redrumm Recordz, Brainstorm Enterprises, Bolaman's TDR, Screwface Records, Big Bert Entertainment, Hoodlife Records, Smugglin' Records, Felonious Records, Rap-A-Lot Records, Red Boy Records, Dean's List Enterprises, Premier Music Group, BooSweet Enterprises, Ophir Entertainment, FVS2 Records, Wall Street Records, Walker Boy Entertainment, Gigantic Entertainment, Blaq Psyircle Entertainment, Imperial Entertainment, Hard Head Records, King B Music, Dee Haywood, Kermit Henderson, Jojo Roberto, Michael Newman, Aaron Burros, Bernd Lichters, Moshe Davenport, Lebron Burros, Greedy Greg, Frances Jones, Jesse Boyce, Chauntey Harvey, Shondale Rounds, Jeremy Miller, Marcus Brown, Dwight Conley, Thomas Pittman, Larry Jones, Judy Foston, Wash Allen, Ronnie Avery, Jose Mangual, Jeruan Lett, Anthony Frazier and many more as there are too many to name. I look forward to many more years of success!

TABLE OF CONTENTS

Opening Scripture – John 10:10 (NKJV)

Closing Scripture - Ezekiel 36:11 (NKJV)

Message from the Author

I have come that they may have life,
and that they may have it more **abundantly**.

John 10:10
NKJV

FOREWORD

It isn't often I'm asked to write about the work of someone who has sat under my teaching. So of course, the natural tendency of the teacher is to scrutinize the work of the student. However, in this case I forgo the natural tendency. I write this to applaud an accomplishment.

I congratulate Michael Matthews for stepping out and presenting his point of view in print – and print lasts forever. He has taken the principles he's learned in life, distilled them and created a potent elixir for those desiring to climb out of the box of the mundane. He tells his story from the viewpoint of the everyday person who dreams to get ahead in life.

Michael, continue to let your enthusiasm be contagious, beckoning others to take their place – their position to receive.

Dr. Ed Montgomery
Houston, Texas

PREFACE

After more than a year of going back and forth with the idea of writing this book, I finally decided this is not just something I simply want to do, it's something I must do! I don't consider myself a writer, an author or by far an expert on the subject of self-help, motivation or even prosperity. I realize there are hundreds, possibly even thousands of books out there that cover these various subjects. Why **Position To Receive** then? The one thing I've notice about self-help, motivation or prosperity books is that they are all written by either wealthy people, preachers, people with PhD's or just simply famous people in general. After all whom does the average person respect, look up to or simply want to hear from? I decided to write **Position To Receive** simply because of that. I firmly believe that it's time for an average person.... someone who doesn't have a PhD, not a preacher, not wealthy and not even close to being famous write about these subjects. Not just write about them, but write about them in a simplistic way that the average person can relate to and can actually apply the same principles to their life! After all, can you relate to the millions and billions that an Oprah or Donald

Trump have. Sure we'd love to hear all the success stories and read about the fascinating lives of people, but come on now, certain things are just out of our league. Most of us will never see that type of lifestyle; much less understand how to even acquire it.

By far, the intent of this book is to explore and share some of the principles, ideas and beliefs I have learned and acquired over the years that have taken me this far in my life. This book is not a typical biography nor do I want it to be. I believe this book is a tangible version of my testimony. One of my biggest aspirations for this book is that it will be a blessing to the reader to the extent that it blows your mind! I want to help bring people to another level in their thinking. I do not claim to know it all, but I firmly believe our purpose in life is to bless others and share what God has blessed us with, not just with things or money, but with knowledge! Anyone that knows me, knows I always say it's not who you know; it's WHAT YOU KNOW to do with WHO YOU KNOW. Everybody knows somebody, but most of us don't know what to do with who we know. This was one of the first real principles I learned in business. How to apply knowledge with whom I know to make things happen as well as who other people know too!

As I write this book, I want to make sure that you understand the true essence of what I'm explaining. I've decided not to hire fancy editors and English professors to make sure everything is grammatically correct. I've decided to keep this book as real as I possibly can, all the way up to the run-on sentences and improper use of some words. I believe when you are really hungry, it's not as important what temperature the food is; what type of food you get or the way it's prepared, all you want is some food! If you choose to continue reading, I promise you will be fed so much to the point where you will be able to feed others!

As you continue reading **Position To Receive**, you'll find a lot of valuable information regarding finances, wealth building systems, unorthodox business principles and philosophies. By no means am I attempting to be a financial advisor, lawyer or spiritual advisor. My intentions are strictly to share my experiences, philosophies and testimonies throughout my walk of life believing that it will motivate and encourage you in your walk. If you are not confident in something, you should always seek professional advice.

Some of the things I talk about in this book may not be a secret to some, but my goal is to share a lot of valuable information that I have discovered with the masses. This book is being offered at a very low price, but yet contains thousands of dollars worth of information and resources. My intent is to level the playing field with information not *availability*. I've found that some of the information contained in this book may be *available* to everyone, but not everyone can afford them. One of the main objectives of **Position To Receive** is to sow into the average person's life an over abundance of knowledge with the belief that they will become an even bigger blessing to others!

I think one of the biggest reasons I had such a hard time with the decision to write this book was God. I wasn't quite sure how to write a book that is not geared solely to the Christian community, but for the world to enjoy. At first I really didn't want to write anything to do with God, thinking it may discourage non-believers from reading it or actually allowing the blessings of this book to flow into their lives. I said I was not going to quote any scriptures, make any references or mention any spiritual-type words, but then after months of looking at a blank page, I realized it is simply impossible to write about any of these subjects without mentioning God in one way or another. That is why this book opens with the scripture John 10:10 - *I have come that they may have life, and that they may have it more abundantly*. If I'm going to write about having abundance and prosperity, I have to start with the source. If you are a non-believer reading this, I ask for your patience and that you would continue reading. It's really funny because I'm around a lot of non-believers in the entertainment industry; and often I find that they practice the principles of God even more than the believers do (of course they just don't know it). Why is it that most successful non-believers grasp so many principles of God, but yet they don't attend a ministry or even believe? I want to challenge you to keep reading these pages and I promise you will be enlightened just the same no matter what your faith is. Who knows? This book may even speak to that inner voice that draws you to an even clearer understanding.

And finally, as I begin sharing pieces of my life and stories of those around me I ask that you keep an open mind as I invite you into my world. This is not a book intended to boast or brag; it is not a book of non-truths or fairy tales but a book of faith, direction and principle. My focus is clear, my purpose is direct and my only goal is to bring the paradigm of the reader to another level, so that you too can improve your personal and professional life!

INTRODUCTION

I can recall a day when I was feeling down and depressed. I really didn't even know what direction I was going in my life. I didn't have fifty cents in my pocket or even a dollar in the bank! I think it was probably one of the lowest times I have ever been in my life. On top of that I was going through a lot of personal problems and I couldn't really focus on the future much less the next ten minutes. Little did I know that the next ten minutes would literally change my life forever? As I was sitting there sulking in my own misery, I was flicking through the channels on the television. It was the middle of the day and nothing was really on but soap operas and game shows. As I was changing the channel something told me to stop. A man was on the television I had never seen or heard of before. His name was Dr. Myles Munroe. As I sat there I began listening to what he was saying. He said "I have a word for all you entrepreneurs! You must find something you are good at... just one thing... you must master it... to master something means to have *dominion* over it!"

Immediately he grabbed my attention. It was as if he was right there in the room talking directly to me and only me! Even though he continued to speak on his message, all I could think about was what he said. At that very moment it dawned on me. For years I had been doing a lot of different things in my business. I really didn't have any particular direction or points of focus. All I knew was I wanted to be successful by having a thriving career and make a lot of money. At the time, this could not be farther from the truth. I had been doing so much yet felt like I was getting nowhere. I was doing the complete opposite of what he said. I was doing a little of everything instead of doing a lot of one thing. It didn't matter whether I was good at it or not. If it was in my field (music business) and I thought it could help my career and make me money I was doing it or trying to at least. It was even to the point where I was doing all these different things under one business. After realizing what I was doing wasn't getting me anywhere and being sick and tired of my situation, I decided to take Dr. Munroe's advice. I looked at everything I was doing and thought about what I was good at… what that one thing was? I looked back over the years and thought what made me money. I thought about what had worked for me and made me feel good. After pondering on that for a few minutes, I determined marketing was my niche. It was something that just came naturally to me. Although I wasn't making any money from it at the time, I had earned money from marketing in the past. I knew it was something I was very good at. There it was right in front of me. "Marketing…." I said to myself, "I'm going to be a master at marketing!" Then I remembered Dr. Munroe saying "to master something means to have *dominion* over it!" At that very moment I clearly heard a voice in my head say, "Dominion…Marketing…" I immediately jumped up, pulled myself together and went to work on forming my new found business, Dominion Marketing….

CHAPTER 1

Finding Your Gift

I think where a lot of people go wrong in life is they haven't found their gift. Sometimes you have to settle down and really analyze what exactly you are good at. People are simply comfortable right where they are in life. They get up everyday and go to work, come home and spend a little time with their family, go to sleep and then repeat it all over again the next day. My wife told me one day, "Most people think their purpose is to work and keep on living. That's not a purpose, that's a function of life." For me, it has taken years to really discover what I'm good at. A very wise man once told me, "If you can market people, you can market anything!" I think from that point on I have been able to focus more on my gifting.

I started off like a lot of people picking various occupations and trying different things that interest me. I first called myself wanting to be a chef, write a cookbook and maybe even have my own cooking show. I used to sit back and watch Yan Can Cook on television and study his unique techniques as he prepared special Asian dishes. I remember kids making fun of me as I was an honor student in Homemaking. I use to go to school early and just hang out in the classroom kitchen. From there I wanted to be a tailor and design clothes for various entertainers. I learned a lot about sewing from my mother and aunt who saw I had a deep passion for sewing and taught me their techniques. I even started taking sewing classes in school and working on some unique designs. At the time I was very young but was very blessed to have my very own model to wear my clothes.... my brother. He was becoming one of the top models in Houston and was building a strong following. It wasn't long before he was wearing all my clothes and some unique designs we spent countless hours coming up with. After a couple years the sewing and the designing began to wear a little thin and the industry was changing drastically. Being so young and not having the resources to go further. I started thinking about what it was I really wanted to do with my life.

 "Most people think their purpose is to work and keep on living. That's not a purpose, that's a function of life."

I think one of the biggest things that helped me find my gift was drive and determination. As a teenager and going through school it's pretty natural to have different interest and wanting to do different things as a career.

But as you start to grow up your thinking begins to change. As I look back and reflect, I didn't really understand what my gift was or what that was even all about. I was just running around doing a lot of stuff. Like most people trying to get a business off the ground I didn't have any money and was still searching for that niche. I was blessed to have my family that supported me and allowed me to pursue my dreams, but I still couldn't quite put my finger on it.

A lot of people say they know what they want to do, but I believe your true gift is something that comes naturally to you. It comes from within you. I mean deep in your heart, not just in your head. I know a lot of people who have gone through years of school and training in a particular field; some may make a decent living and yet are just not very happy. The side that people don't really talk about is the percentage of people that go through all the training and years of schooling and still can't find a job! I'm not saying don't go to school or not to seek training for a particular trade, I'm simply suggesting you may want to seek your true gifting first and then pursue further development and training.

For me finding my gift was revealed more and more as I dreamed. I think a lot of people in life don't know how to dream. Some people are even scared to dream. Most people just get too comfortable too fast. Nothing drives them, nothing motivates them to dream. I don't think I've ever been one to just be that comfortable. It's just not me! Like most people one of my motivations was money. Growing up not really having much money played a role in my drive and determination. I know some people who don't have much and still have no drive and determination. For some people, I don't know what it's going to take. I think my biggest motivation was I simply did not want to work for someone else. Of course the American Dream as they say is to own your own business, but for me it was much more. Ever since I was little I've always had the mindset of there is your AT&T's, Southwestern Bell's, Mary Kay's etc, why can't there be an MJM (my initials)? I don't just want to have a business but I want to have an entire network. Have you ever thought about how much money these types of companies make from other people dreaming? These companies are literally built on things like multi-level marketing and people that are content with making someone else rich for only a small piece of the pie. I'm not saying there's anything wrong with this but my philosophy has always been why I can't build my own network versus contributing to someone else's. Sometimes you can't be afraid to dream and dream big! Don't let finances, lack of education, experience, race or anything else be an excuse! When you're not sure of your purpose and gifting, it's often difficult on where to begin. I want to challenge you to step out of your comfort zone and discover a world of gifts through dreaming. That's what I did and so can you!

CHAPTER 2

Start-Up Mindset

No matter what you decide to do in life make sure you focus on your niche. I think that one of the biggest problems I encountered was when I was doing too many things. I am so glad I turned on the television that day and heard Dr. Myles Munroe. As he said, "find one thing and take dominion over it!" Whatever it is you decide to do make sure you stay focused and don't get caught up doing all these wonderful things to only reap little results. Be sure you are happy and comfortable in what you are doing and that you acquire a full understanding of what you're getting into.

I can remember starting up with just a basic black and white business card from Office Depot and a black and white flyer brochure detailing more than one hundred services. I really thought I was doing something, that I was building a real business. I figured if I learned a lot about everything and did everything I possibly can, I would be more successful and make lots of money. Little did I know all I was doing was what I now call running around in it. Everybody has to start somewhere and with something, right? Like most, this was a starting platform for me to build my business on as I found my niche.

I think the biggest thing most people are concerned with when trying to get off the ground is money. Most people have great ideas but are often discouraged because they don't have the resources to get it going much less take it to the next level. I refuse to let that be my excuse. I tried to focus more on adjusting my mindset than the need for money. After all, you don't have the start-up money, so what else do you have besides a bright idea?

 I tried to focus more on adjusting my mindset than the need for money.

I remember one day I was having real bad financial problems. Business was real slow and things just didn't seem to be going right. Nothing I did was working in my favor. My economic situation was just horrible! Checks were bouncing in my bank account, the overdraft fees where piling up, man it seemed like I could barely keep up with my bills, let alone keep food on the table. As I sulked in my own misery, I recalled hearing a voice tell me to "go buy bigger checks." I thought I was losing my mind, it was crazy. I was like what's happening now, am I hearing things? As with most people I had the standard size wallet checks, you know the ones that either came free with your checking account or for a minimal fee like $9.99 or something. I started to think, "I can't afford big checks... I'm bouncing the small checks I have right now. Those big checks cost a lot of money!" and money at the time was something I just didn't have. Besides, what would I do with big checks, after all a check is a check right? Well as I was quick to dismiss the idea; I didn't realize at the time that God was working on my mindset. A few days later, I went to check the mailbox. As I was going through the junk mail, there was a flyer that stood out to me. It was big checks at reduced prices by a company called Checkcrafters. There it was right in front of me... big checks for nineteen dollars and ninety-five cents! I couldn't believe my eyes, those same size checks at my bank cost seventy-five to a hundred dollars easy! I immediately thought to myself this is absolutely crazy, here I was just the other day hearing a voice telling me to go and buy big checks, and now I get offered big checks that I can actually afford. At this point I wasn't so quick to dismiss the idea. After thinking about it for a second I said, "What do I have to lose? This has got to be some kind of sign!" To make a long story short, from that day forward I'm proud to say, I have never bounced another check again!

As I reflect back, I share that story about the big checks because many of us have heard that inner voice and have chosen to ignore it, just like I did at first. I'm so thankful to have been given a second chance when the brochure came to me. It's all about a certain type of mindset you must have. I want to write big amounts, so why not have big checks? This is just one example of adjusting your mindset to increase your situation and broaden your thought process.

I often think, "Why did it take me so many years to get my mindset right?" I remember when I first started off as a business consultant, again just one of those hundreds of services I was providing at the time. I use to charge five-hundred dollars a month to consult with companies. During that time period, I was in the mind frame of trying to keep food on the table and the bills paid like most people. After consulting with many companies for several years, I began to start thinking about how hard I was working and how much of my time I was giving up, only to get a little in return. Was I really getting anywhere? I mean career wise, was I advancing towards reaching my goals? Like most people, I was caught up in what I call "the comfort zone." Only when I began to feel frustrated and overworked, did I start to think about what I've been doing the whole time. Although years had gone by and I needed to seriously change my situation if I was going to get back on track!

One Sunday as I was sitting it church, my pastor started talking about a scripture in Luke 11:9 (NKJV) "So I say to you ask, and it will be given to you;" I reflected on my situation and started thinking to myself, "I need to *ask* for more money." As I thought about this more and more, I figured what really was it that I had to lose. So the next potential client I had, I tried asking for two thousand dollars instead of my usual five hundred dollars. I know that sounds like a big jump, but after careful review of all the work I was doing, that still really wasn't enough. Sure enough after I asked, they said okay to my terms and started paying me two thousand dollars per month. This was a major turning point in my mindset because here I was now being paid three times as much for the same amount of work. The reality was now I didn't need to take on as many clients, which freed up more of my time. Who would have thought a simple little three letter word, *ask* would be so powerful?

 Who would have thought a simple little three letter word, *ask* would be so powerful?

I hate to think if only I would have heard that one word from God years earlier what would've happened. What would my *position* be like? Sometimes in life we simply have to *ask* for what it is we want. I mean really get a little more aggressive. After all what do we have to lose? The worst case scenario is that all someone can say is no, right? But what if they say yes? I know this sound crazy, but I encourage you to try asking for yourself and see what happens. Who knows, you just might get it!

CHAPTER 3

Position To Receive

I think one of the best mindsets anyone can have is to be "future based." It took me years to understand what this actually is all about. I think for most people we are in the mindset of today and today only. People are generally focused on just having a good time and enjoying life for today. How does it go? Live for today cause tomorrow isn't promised. I wonder what the world would be like if everyone thought like that. Being "future based" is something I feel needs to be talked about more in today's society. Nobody worries about the future anymore. I remember growing up people talked about further education, building businesses, leaving something for their children and the days of retirement. Now you generally hear more about things like I can't afford education, don't have the money to grow and build my business, I can barely take care of things now much less put anything away for my children, there's not going to be any social security anyway and I don't have any retirement. I believe one of the scariest moments I ever experienced in my life was when I thought about the future. I know that sounds bizarre, but it was real crazy. I recall one day I was sitting around my house and a thought popped in my head, "What about this time next year? How am I going to make it?" I literally almost passed out! I had to catch myself. I felt faint; it was almost like I instantly became ill. I will never forget that moment. Why would a simple thought about this time next year be so traumatic? I couldn't believe it. I didn't want to believe it. All kinds of thoughts ran through my head. How am I going to pay my bills then? I'm already living month to month like most people. I can just barely pay this month's mortgage payment, much less how I'm going to pay it twelve months from now. What if my wife got sick? I don't have any insurance or medical benefits. What if I wasn't able to physically work anymore? I don't have any savings or any type of safety net. All types of crazy thoughts started running through my head! I just couldn't see it. I couldn't even imagine it. I think that's really what bothered me the most; I didn't have anything for the future. No type of security whatsoever. Most people are so busy living for today; they are not even concerned about tomorrow much less the distant future. I think from that point on, I've been very determined to work on being future based. I look at today's society and so many people are dying so young. Lately the average age range of death you tend to hear the most about is 18-36. Is that even considered a generation? A very wise man once told me, "Young people are dying young because they are stressed out just by trying to keep up with everybody else! They're not worried about maintaining, they're more concerned with trying to out do one another and have all these wonderful things! They feel they have to hustle ten times harder. The way society puts everything in their face, it's like you must have this or that. It's simply ridiculous! And they wonder why people are dying young. They're over stressed!" That's a conversation I will never forget, it was actually a big wake up call for me. I actually looked at myself to make sure I wasn't caught up in that very same stereotype. It's so easy in today's society to get caught up, before you know it you are in too deep or it's just simply too late. Everyone is so focused on having things now, the demand dictates that yesterday you where suppose to have it and if you don't you're behind somehow. I don't really get it and the sad part about it is they're not even thinking about having anything for the future.

 Everyone is so focused on having things now... they're not even thinking about having anything for the future.

How can one really start to look at the future when you can't really see past the present? The answer is simple... you've got to get yourself into the **Position To Receive**. That's what I did. I'm going to speak about the financial aspect first. Although I don't work a regular nine to five, I try to put myself in the mindset of an average worker. If you work a regular job the only increases you tend to see is maybe a pay raise or possibly a bonus check that's pretty much about it. See that's part of the problem, there really isn't any room for increase. In order to get into the **Position To Receive** you have to have something in place that will enable you to have *endless possibilities*. I'm not saying quit your job. See, if your job will only allow you to work forty hours a week or doesn't give any bonuses; no matter how hard you work, your pay check will always be the same. This is why a lot of workers simply just do the basic requirements of their job. Sure if you're a hard worker, there may be a chance of a promotion with a pay raise, but at the same time be realistic, how often is that going to happen? What is it once, twice a year maybe? This is the story for most people. I believe its part of the problem that plays a role in the "comfort zone" theory. People generally are lazy and don't want to do more than they have to. So if they feel all they will get is forty hours worth of pay no matter how hard they work, that's pretty much what they will focus on. They automatically limit themselves to a forty hour work week. See, in the self-employed realm there is no hourly pay! We can work for hours, maybe even days and not make a dime! Some people can't even imagine what that would be like. Why would anyone want to do that you ask? Well for starters the belief system is very different, when you don't have a steady pay check coming every week or every other week, you don't have any time frame, no forty hour confinement and you simply understand if you don't work, you don't eat! There are no time restraints when it comes to your work day. You also know that there are *endless possibilities* to what you can earn because you're not working on an hourly wage or flat salary type pay. After all, there are only so many hours in a day! The more you work it increases your chances of making more money when you are self-employed. The thought process is very different between the two. Many times the self-employed think about getting themselves in the **Position To Receive** more than an average worker; mainly because of the lack of overall security. Many times there are no benefits; and like I said before there is no pay check every week or every other week!

 In order to get into the Position To Receive you have to have something in place that will enable you to have *endless possibilities*.

There are many things one can do to get themselves into the **Position To Receive**. You have to think about what exactly you can do that will open yourself up to *endless opportunities* or get involved with something that doesn't limit the money you can make. For example, I turned to the internet. For many years the internet has been around and people have been making huge sums of money on the internet. It is something that doesn't limit you to time confinements, as it's an around the clock thing. It doesn't sleep or stop working like we do. It doesn't limit you to a particular area or any type of demographics whatsoever. The internet I feel is an excellent tool anyone can use to get them in *position;* especially if you work a regular job, due to time restraints. There are hundreds, possibly even thousands of things you can do on the internet to make money. Some people have opened up even dollar stores, travel agencies, referral services and a lot more on the internet. I once met a man in the Las Vegas airport that told me his friend had a business on the internet selling socks! Yes, socks! I couldn't believe it, who would want to pay for socks on the internet? He said something very interesting to me; he said "You'll be surprised what people are willing to buy out there!" I never really thought about it like that. There was even a guy I know selling cars on the internet. He said, "There's a big market for car sales from the South because of the snow in the North." He sells cars on the internet full time, that's his actual job! There is virtually everything for sale online. Just check out EBAY and other auction type sites, if you haven't already. All types of products and services are available on the internet! Another person told me they sell old computer parts that there job throws away on EBAY and they make a lot of extra money. The difference is that the possibilities are endless with the internet! Unlike a store front in a particular city, the most customers they can possible ever have is the population of the city. And let's be honest, no business has the entire population of a city patronizing their business. With the internet there are no limitations, in any way shape or form! It's just that simple.

 There are hundreds, possibly even thousands of things you can do on the internet to make money.

For me, I decided to start my own digital delivery service (of music to djs); it works much like the post office! Instead of sending music by post office to djs on compact disc, we send it digitally via email. At first, I wasn't sure if anyone would be interested in such a service much less pay for it. I decided to start with selling a service instead of a product because I felt it would be less competitive and of course I didn't have to deal with things like inventory, preparing orders and shipping of actual products. I stepped out completely by faith and decided to launch www.looking4airplay.com. That was in the year two-thousand five; I did not know I would become one of the pioneers to bring digital delivery of music as a marketing service to the forefront. Now there are digital delivery services of music popping up all over the country! You see with my internet business, I have *positioned* myself to make money around the clock and have opened my market up worldwide. There is no downtime, no limitations to the money I can make or how many customers I can possibly have. By just starting this type of business through the internet, I put myself is a certain *position*. Even though when I started there were no clients or immediate money, just by starting it, I opened a door to *endless possibilities*! You have to think bigger than just by the hour or an annual bonus check! Think *endless possibilities*! Every morning when I wake up I check my email by complete faith, not knowing if anyone will ever utilize my service or not. But because I have *positioned* myself, I've opened the door to the possibility someone; somewhere will eventually use my service. Through this business, I've learned a lot about probability and how it plays a roll in financial blessing and generating business. If you reach a certain number of people, regardless of your service or product, someone will move on it. That's just the way life is. Everyone buys into a service or idea at some point in their life. Don't ever forget there is a market out there for everyone and everything. The only difference will be how big or small the market size actually is. The vital key is to find out how many potential clients or customers you have to target in order to close the deal or generate the desired amount of business! In time like with anything, as you set yourself up you will learn what the keys are and which one fits in what door!

 Even though when I started there were no clients or immediate money, just by starting it, I opened a door to *endless possibilities*!

In the coming chapters, I'm going to be talking about the many ways you can get yourself into the **Position To Receive**; whether it is through financial rewards, giving back, spiritual growth or wealth building. Whatever it is you choose to do with your life, the main thing is that you get yourself in *position*, so that you can *receive* the abundance of all that's in store for you!

CHAPTER 4

Blessed To Be A Blessing

I believe the most powerful way to get into the **Position To Receive** is to sow a seed. By giving we are opening up the atmosphere around us to *receive*. I'm not just talking about sowing money, although that is a big focus because most of us want to *receive* money. You have to sow whatever it is you are trying to reap. I never really understood this powerful principle until I actually started practicing it. I think one of the hardest things to do in life is to give something to someone who has everything. I mean think about it, if you where going to give something to someone who has everything, millions of dollars in the bank, fancy cars, big house with everything in it and everything their heart desires. What's left? What would you give them? It's very easy to give something to someone who doesn't have anything. Whether it is food to a homeless person or money to someone in dire straits, ask yourself what would you give to someone that has everything? Or better yet, would you even give anything at all? Can you see yourself giving Bill Gates a hundred dollars? How about a thousand to Oprah Winfrey or Donald

Trump? Some people just can't conceive the thought because these people don't need it. Although, the chances they ever will need it is slim; most people's attitude is why they should give them something because they are so wealthy.

 You have to sow whatever it is you are trying to reap. I never really understood this powerful principle until I actually start practicing it.

I remember attending a music conference and there were more than five hundred or so people in a panel forum. Blue Williams, personal manager of a very successful rap group named Outkast, actor Nick Cannon and the CEO of a multi-million dollar company called Family Tree was speaking. There was a young man who got up to ask a question, well at least we thought he was but actually decided to take the opportunity to plug his book on the music business. Anyway, to make a long story short, Mr. Williams asked him to bring him a copy of the book so he can see how much the young man knew. He also asked him who all he managed and what qualified him to write such a book. The young man replied, "I haven't managed nobody, I just gathered information from conferences like this one and decided to put it in a book." Before the panel was over, Mr. Williams had looked over the book and decided to speak on it before ending the panel. He said these simple words, "This kid knows what he's talking about, and I'm going to buy a couple books." Right then and there as Mr. Williams sowed into his life, people from everywhere started surrounding him to purchase his book. He couldn't give his book away before this had taken place. He must have sold at least twenty or thirty books on the spot, if not more at thirty dollars each! As the panel wrapped up, I walked up to the young man and said, "If you're smart you will go bless that man with some of that money you just made!" He just looked at me in disbelief like I didn't just say what I said. You see he couldn't conceive giving a multi-millionaire a few dollars of what he was just blessed with. I explained to him, "If that man didn't just speak a *word* on your behalf, you would have never sold those books!" Needless to say, the young man never did give Mr. Williams anything, not even a thank you. The endorsement could have been priceless, but all the young man was worried about was a few dollars he had made. This type of mindset is exactly why people struggle today. Just think what if the young man would have put a hundred or two in the hands of Mr. Williams? The impact it could have made, even though he didn't need it. He might have been blown away and said he's going to help this young man sell thousands of these books by endorsing him on a larger platform or invest into taking it to another whole level, who knows? But one thing's for sure the moment is gone and we will never find out. This is something I could not live with, how about you? The not knowing... the uncertainty, if I only would step out there and do something that's not easy. Try giving something to someone who has a lot already. Someone who doesn't really need it, especially if they have already blessed your life? I challenge you to try it, go above and beyond and see what happens!

What if you don't have *anything* to give? Most people tend to look at the *thing* as being money or a tangible item of some kind. I can think of one of the most powerful and greatest *things* we all have to give, and that is a *word*. Sometimes all we have to do is sow a *word* in someone's life. Whether it is a *word* of encouragement, knowledge, direction or wisdom, a *word* to uplift, build and open the mind of others. It all started with a *word*, when Mr. Williams spoke up on the behalf of the young man and his book. Then he became blessed! You see it's very rarely anyone speaks up on the behalf of someone. Very rare! Sure a lot of people will say I know of him or her, but will they go to bat and speak on their character and actually endorse them and stand behind them! It just doesn't really happen in society these days. How many times has it happened in your life? I think we can all count on one hand, how many times it has actually taken place. Simply put, I think this is so sad.

 I can think of one of the most powerful and greatest *things* we all have to give, and that is a *word*.

Anything you actually want out of life I believe you will have to sow into it. Whether it is of your time, money, ability, patience or anything else you have to sow into it. I often think about how I got to the point of knowing so much about the business of music. I have to honestly say I never went to school for the trade or read a lot of books on the subject of music. I simply sowed into in. I spent countless hours talking about the business of music. I talked to both people who knew about the business and those that didn't know much. You might be thinking; why would anyone want to talk to someone who doesn't know much about something? I do it because I find they ask very good questions due to the lack of understanding. My greatest challenges come from the inexperienced. This pushes me to the extent if I don't know the answer I have to go find it. I also found out something very interesting happens when I sow what I know about the business to others and others sowed what they knew to me. I often find myself talking about things in a certain way that I have to catch myself. Sometimes I didn't even realize I knew what I even said or in that specific way I referred to it. Has that ever happened to you? Its incredible how in just dwelling on something can actually bring something out of you, that you didn't know was there. It was actually there the whole time. Now that's powerful! My pastor talked about something similar to this one time he said, "It's like calling for a pizza, whenever you decide to call to order a pizza, you just call and place your order. The pizza may not be made yet, but all the ingredients are already there to make it.

st calling forth for something you already
re!"

ching a DVD one day about a documentary on
hip-hop mogul Russell Simmons, and the interviewer
asked him, "Why do you do what you do?" Russell
simply replied, "To serve..." You see as one of the few
African American billionaires in the entertainment
business, much less the world, he understands the
power of giving, that we are blessed to be a blessing.
Sure you might say, well he's in the *position* to give;
after all he's a billionaire! Well although I've had the
privilege to meet Mr. Simmons and talk with him one
on one, it wasn't until I watched the DVD that day, I
really felt like I understood why he's even in the
position to begin with. I had always respected him for
his business savvy, but I had no true idea why he's been
so successful until that day. He further explained, "How
you think is where you're going!" See, it's all about
one's mindset. Despite knowing what he knows about
the entertainment business, he chooses to give back
constantly by having a lot of interns around him,
educating and sharing his wisdom with others and using
his influence with people to raise money for charities
and other types of fundraisers. He's constantly giving
away free clothes and tennis shoes from his clothing
line, Phat Farm. Mr. Simmons also stated, "If you want
to be rich you have to help somebody make money!
You will never have nothing unless you *give* first.
Giving is the basis of all success period!"

I was flicking through the television and landed on the channel that was airing the life story of comedian, Steve Harvey. As they interviewed him he began to explain how he's managed to be very successful and make lots of money. He explained how he has bought a bunch of nice things and all that. He said, "It's not about all that anymore, it's about *giving* back and helping someone else. He's trying to find his purpose in life and he wants to feel like he's doing something and making a difference." This is really the foundation of the whole **Position To Receive** book, it's about *giving* back and pouring into people's lives some of what I've been blessed to *receive*. Even as you read this, part of the proceeds of this book is being given to Abundant Life Cathedral ministries and my pastor, Dr. Ed Montgomery. See its all about the flow of blessings! Once you truly understand the *giving* principle, only then will you truly *position* yourself in the cycle to *receive*.

"If you want to be rich you have to help somebody make money! You will never have nothing unless you *give* first. *Giving* is the basis of all success period!"
- Russell Simmons

CHAPTER 5

How Big Is Your Nothing?

I remember one Sunday while sitting in church my pastor started his sermon by asking everyone to open their Bible to Matthew 17:20. As we all turned to it, I began reading to myself. It said, "Because of your unbelief; for assuredly, I say to you, if you have faith as a mustard seed, you will say to this mountain, Move from here to there, and it will move; and *nothing* will be impossible for *you*." I don't know about you, but as I was growing up I can recall hearing people always say things like "nothing's too hard for God, there's nothing God can't do, and there's nothing to big for God". I never really thought about it a whole lot until that day about what that scripture actual says *"Nothing* will be impossible for *you*." Most people don't actually believe this. People don't generally go around saying things like *nothing* is impossible for *me*! It just doesn't seem normal. You see it's easy for anyone to say "Nothing is impossible for God", but that's not what it says. It says, *"Nothing* will be impossible for *you*." I believe the reason people don't believe this is because they have a hard time seeing themselves on God's level. Try it, go

ahead say it "Nothing is impossible for me!" See that
wasn't too hard. Now if we can just really believe it
deep down inside. I think if we all reflect on our lives,
at some point we can give a testimony of something
we've made it through or achieved that was considered
to be impossible at the time!

 "...and *nothing* will be impossible for *you*."
Matthew 17:20 (NKJV)

Just when I thought I was thinking deep about what the
scripture said, my pastor asked the question, "How big
is your nothing?" I felt as though he was talking
directly to me. I actually had to go back and re-read it
again. What a powerful question? Its one thing to
believe *nothing* is impossible for *you*, it's entirely
another to think about the size of the *nothing*. This goes
back to having the right mindset. No matter what it is
you are focused on achieving, you have to believe you
can do it. Don't let the size of it stand in your way or
anything else for that matter.

I can use this book as a prime example; I am not a
professional writer. I've never written anything longer
than a book report; and now I'm going to share my
thoughts and beliefs in a book with the world. I don't
know anything about publishing a book, not a clue;
don't know anything about the book industry outside of
a local bookstore, yet I am writing this very book in
your hands. The simple fact that you are reading this
right now could have been considered impossible for

me before. Who knows what the future holds? **Position To Receive** could even become a best seller one day. It can go on to touch the lives of many people around the world. Can you believe it in the same breath I'm saying I'm not a professional writer, but yet God has already given me the ideas for my next two books? They are going to be called **Position To Receive Too!** and **Self-Made** which will be available in a few years after this one is released. And can you believe it I haven't even finished this one yet. I told you what happens when you change your mindset, *nothing* is impossible!

I recently sat down for a meeting with a well known author for some insight and direction. I said to him, "I am not writing this book for money, fame, to sign autographs or to be on television?" He simply replied, "Why not?" I told him that wasn't my purpose or intent for this book. You see, even using myself as an example, I did what most people do, I limited my own possibilities. We can not fully *receive* everything that is in store for us if we continue to limit ourselves.

 We can not fully *receive* everything that is in store for us if we continue to limit ourselves.

As you think about your life and the things you want to achieve, remember *nothing* is impossible for *you*. Don't get caught up in the limitations of your natural thought process. Try to think beyond the scope of your reach and challenge yourself to rise up above what's merely possible. If you find yourself in disbelief remember to step back and ask yourself, "How big is your *nothing*?"

CHAPTER 6

Another Level Faith

As I think about the world today much is changing so rapidly. Cost of living is just sky rocketing! Gas prices are going through the roof, food prices are soaring, insurance is on the rise and everyday utilities are at an all time high. What is the world coming to? The worst part about it is people aren't even making more money! Sometimes I sit back and think about how people are making it everyday. I wonder especially about those in that "comfort zone". I often think maybe all this is happening to literally shake up people's mindsets and open their eyes to get themselves in *position*. I think in order to survive in today's world you have to have what I call another level of faith! No longer can you simply rely solely on the natural, them days are over. Whether you are a believer or not you must have some type of faith if you're going to survive. Faith is believing in something or for something even though you can not see it in the natural. Having what I call is another level of faith is where you can't see it and will continue to believe for it; even if you never get it.

This is something that is very hard to do. It takes a lot of patience, discipline and true passion. I think when you really want something so bad and you're genuinely hungry for it, another level of faith comes a lot easier. No matter what the outcome is you'll still believe because of that deep down burning desire for it. Have you tested your levels of faith lately?

Being an entrepreneur, we tend to live by another level of faith constantly. At times you don't know when you'll get your next client, make that next sale or when the next customer will walk through the door. It simply takes another level of faith to live from day to day; week to week; month to month; year to year, especially under those types of conditions.

 I think when you really want something so bad and you're genuinely hungry for it, another level of faith comes a lot easier.

I believe you have to start with the basics of faith. Like with brakes in a car, everyone that drives exercises a certain level of faith. For example when you go to apply the brakes in your car and the car comes to a stop. We sometimes take it for granted; it's like second nature, we just believe every time we put our foot on the brake, the car will stop. Now that takes basic faith.

Part of getting yourself into the **Position To Receive** requires another level of faith. You can not be afraid to take risks and try something new. Sometimes you just have to step out of the box. Sometimes you have to go against the grain, be innovative and challenge yourself and others too. I know for most people this can be difficult to do, especially those in the "comfort zone". That is exactly why another level of faith is required. I often hear people say, "Well I'd rather not be bothered or I'm not comfortable with this or that." I think sometimes we have to do something different if we want different results. That's the key right there; you have to want different results! You simply can not be afraid to step out and learn something new, try something different and see where your faith takes you. Buckle up, the ride isn't always smooth. It's not always about how the smooth the ride is; it's about reaching your destination!

 I think sometimes we have to do something different if we want different results.

I remember when I first started my internet business, looking4airplay.com. I was very nervous because I didn't know anything about running an internet business. I didn't have a clue about how to build websites, the internet lingo or anything; much less how to market online. I was totally ignorant to the whole cyberspace thing. I had to step out by complete faith and nothing but faith. I had to believe that if I spend the initial money it took to get it going, did my research on every aspect and put the work into it; the business would be successful. I call myself a late bloomer when it comes to the internet. I say this because it's been around for a couple decades now and I'm just now getting into it. As I launched the business back in 2005, who would have thought in its first year it would gross one thousand percent profit? Imagine if I would have started years earlier? See, this is why it is important we exercise another level of faith. We are supposed to have everything that God wants us to have. We really need to stop limiting ourselves by not using our faith. Most importantly I feel we also limit God when we're not exercising our faith. Sometimes we have to stretch ourselves a little bit more, go the extra distance. I call it put your hands to work and then God will get into it. Many times we don't want to get down and get our hands dirty. Don't you think it's time we stepped our faith up?

 We really need to stop limiting ourselves by not using our faith.

It takes another level of faith to give money especially when you do not have it to give. This can be the best time to exercise another level of faith. It's easy to give when you have it, but what about when you don't? Sometimes we have to stretch onto another level of faith and trust God no matter what, especially in the tough economic times. Show him that no matter what you are going through economically, you are going to give even if it's your last! What you're doing is putting your absolute trust in him. I know someone who was down economically to his last few dollars. Business had been real slow for him and it seemed as though financially nothing was working out. He decided one day while attending church, he would sow all that he had left into the offering. He felt as if he already was down, he wasn't going to be able to pay any of his bills anyway or anything else for that matter. He decided to put his complete trust in God and exercise another level of faith that God will provide. After a couple days, business all of a sudden picked up and he started to get back on feet economically, not just providing finances to take care of his bills but to continue to sow even more than before!

Another level of faith can be very difficult to understand when you haven't really gone through things in life. I think we all can relate to wanting something so bad and you can't quite seem to get your hands on it. One thing is to simply believe for something to happen and another is to keep believing for it regardless to what happens! It's that above and beyond faith! It's the drive and determination to go the complete distance no matter how long something takes or how difficult it may be. That's another level of faith! Don't you think it's time you stepped up your faith to another level and begin opening new doors of opportunities? I challenge you to test the levels of your faith and believe for things you never imagined before. As you begin to expand your faith and with the right mindset there is *nothing* you can't accomplish!

It's that above and beyond faith! It's the
drive and determination to go the
complete distance no matter how long
something takes or how difficult it may
be. That's another level of faith!

CHAPTER 7

Teachable

I don't know what it is exactly, but I've come to the realization you can't tell people what to do or how to do it. No matter what it is you know about in life it's very hard to tell anyone anything these days. I'm sure we can all remember growing up and our parents use to tell us not to do this and not to do that. We use to just let it go in one ear and out the other. After all isn't that a part of growing up? Only to later on in life admit that we probably should have just listened in the first place. And most of the time we only want to admit it, if we were in trouble, got caught up or things didn't work out as we expected. I heard someone say, "The best lesson learned, is a bought lesson". I'm not quite sure if I agree with that. My concern is why pay for it in the first place? You have so many people that continue to pay for lessons and still haven't learned a thing. Some are even willing to pay for more! I've come to the understanding if you want to be successful in life you simply just have to be teachable.

You have to really ask yourself are you teachable? Are you the type of person that thinks they know it all? Are you the type of person that doesn't like anyone to tell them anything, no matter what it's about? Have you allowed yourself to be open enough to receive? I recall one Sunday at church; my pastor began breaking down authority. He said, "In order to be in authority, you must submit to authority!" I think it really took me awhile to get a full understanding of that statement. Most of us want to be in authority, but have never submitted to authority. There is nothing in life that someone, somewhere hasn't already experienced. So why do we think we have to learn for ourselves? I still can't figure that one out.

 There is nothing in life that someone, somewhere hasn't already experienced.

I think a lot of being teachable is all about discipline. As you figure out your purpose and goals in life you have to submit to it. What I mean by submit is open yourself up to it. Absorb everything you can about every aspect of it like a sponge soaking up every drop of a spill. Don't hold on to just what you know; look for what it is you don't know. I think about it like an experienced lawyer reading over a contract. The lawyer tends to focus not just on what the contract says but what it doesn't say too, so all aspects are fully covered. This can make all the difference.

A lot of what you're reading in this book is because I've allowed myself to be teachable. I've learned that people naturally like to speak about what it is they do. You'll be surprised at what people are willing to share with you, if you just listen and allow yourself to be teachable. The unique thing about being in the music business is that you meet a lot of interesting people in many different fields. Some of my clients have been in real estate, medical doctors, lawyers, professional athletes and even Wall Street stock traders. Over the years I have been privilege to walk with some very successful people whom have shared so much with me simply because I was teachable.

 You'll be surprised at what people are willing to share with you, if you just listen and allow yourself to be teachable.

I remember one day while I was visiting at a client's home. I couldn't help but notice a work station in the middle of his living room. I saw something very unusual to me a computer with four monitors. Naturally I wasn't trying to be nosy but I couldn't help but ask, "Why do you need four monitors to operate your computer?" He laughed and said, "Sit down, and let me show you" While the computer was booting up he said, "You do what you do with the music thing, I do what I do with stocks!" He began asking me if I ever heard of option trading and was I familiar with the stock market. That was the first time I was really introduced to option trading. I really didn't know too much about the stock market either. As I showed interest in what he was doing he began to share with me information about it. After talking about the stock market for awhile he began explaining to me, "I may not know anything about the music business, but I can guarantee you that Wall Street and the stock market isn't going anywhere!" Then he clicked the mouse button and said "that's another twenty grand!" I think at that very moment I was sold. I couldn't believe my eyes. I quickly asked, "Where do I begin? How can I get involved with trading?" He said, "Go open a TD Waterhouse account (now TDAmeritrade) and I'll teach you." To make a long story short, I went on to become an occasional option trader, making money from day trading options and have now taught others how to do it. All of this happened simply because I was teachable.

 As I showed interest in what he was doing he began to share with me information about it.

You see if I hadn't of allowed myself to be teachable I would have never learned something new. I would have missed a blessing. Not just the financial blessings of option trading but being able to bless others too! One thing he had said I will never forget, "No matter if you lose money or not, the one thing nobody can ever take away from you is the knowledge of how to do it!" I think that is what being teachable is all about; gaining that knowledge that no one can ever take away!

There are two types of voices I would like to focus on. One is God's voice within us and the other is God's voice through other people. I want to share with you a simple technique I use that allows me to hear God's voice within me. Like most people my life is filled with a lot of distractions and complications that often makes it hard to hear. One thing I discovered that allows me to hear God's voice clearly is simply to speak with others about a particular subject for a long period of time. How many times have you had a conversation and then afterwards saying to yourself, I can't believe I just said that or I didn't know I knew that? It's quite remarkable how God works through us, if we just give him a chance. I find a lot of valuable information that we need is already within us. We just have to find a way to draw it out. Sometimes we have to be patient. This is something that's hard for many of us to do. We may have to keep talking about something over and over again till things just start coming out. I know this sounds crazy but it actually works, if you haven't experienced this for yourself, give it a try and see what happens, after all what do you have to lose. You might just surprise yourself!

 It's quite remarkable how God works through us, if we just give him a chance.

The ability to hear God's voice through other people is a little more difficult. I think mainly because we tend to trust ourselves more than we trust other people. I truly believe God speaks through everyone, most of the time we just don't pay attention, especially if we are distracted, don't like the person or simply don't want to hear it. I think if we keep ourselves in a mode to *receive*, we can hear a lot more clearly. In business, you'll find most people will volunteer a lot of information if you are just willing to listen. Try talking to more people and asking a lot of questions, so you can draw out God's voice in them as well as God's voice in you.

CHAPTER 9

Make People Rich

Over the years I learned a very important lesson in business. That lesson is you can never be afraid to make people rich! Most people tend to focus on how much money other people make. I think this was one of my biggest mistakes early on in business. Many times we lose opportunities to make money behind worrying about someone else's pocket.

There is a big difference in this area in the mindset of an entrepreneur and the average working class person. The average working class person simply goes to work, do their job and get paid an hourly wage or salary. They do not generally focus on how much money they make the employer or the company. With entrepreneurs they may contract out services or provide the service themselves. If they hire independent contractors or service providers they may look at how much the other party is making, possibly even compare it to what they are making. This is a big mistake. Simply put, if it wasn't for the other party you wouldn't make what you are going to make. I think the philosophy of making people rich is the start of making yourself rich! A lot of my service providers with my business often ask me, why I tell them I want to make them rich. I simply tell them because if they're rich, I'm rich. Think about it, the more money they make is the more money I make. We all know money motivates people and if you can keep those motivated around you, they will make you rich!

For most of us, we don't own anything we're just running around in it. What I mean by that is until we understand the real objective at hand we can not be successful. I know a lot of people that try to focus on owning everything. Most of them tend to fail because their focus for owning is wrong. I talked to a guy one day that cleans windows for a living. I asked him, "Why don't you start your own window cleaning business?" He replied, "I use to years ago, but I got tired of all the long hours, paperwork and the headache that comes with ownership! Now I'm comfortable just doing my job, making my money and going home at five o'clock, not having to worry about nothing else." You've got to make sure if you plan to own that you are prepared for everything that comes with it. Owning your own business is not for everybody!

Having tried both the product and the service type businesses, I found that service oriented businesses seem to work the best for me. You have to decide what works for you, if you're going to own your own business. I'm not saying that you can't make money selling products, many people do. Some people are just natural sales people and can sell ice to an Eskimo. I know some people who make a lot of money selling cars, Mary Kay make-up, houses and even beauty supplies. But when it all boils down to it, they don't own any of it. Someone above them is making that initial dollar. I know it sounds selfish to think about being the top dog, but why not? What's wrong with wanting to be the person at the top, instead of simply being in someone's down line. I think that's part of the problem, a lot of people think too small, they're satisfied with being whatever place they can get in. It all leads back to ones mindset, where do you want to be... at the top... in the middle... or at the bottom of the totem pole. The choice is yours.

 Owning your own business is not for everybody!

When I started my CD and DVD manufacturing business, I couldn't imagine how easy it would be to make money. For years, I had always referred my clients to manufacturing plants or simply asked them to provide us with the product. Then after talking to some people in the manufacturing business one day, they explained to me how lucrative it could be for me. They said based upon how much volume of business I was referring away to others and the fact I was not receiving any commissions for it, I really got to thinking. They also explained to me I could receive broker rates and start my own business. That I can actually sell the product at end user or retail pricing and make a decent profit off of each job and not have to invest in any equipment, staff, warehouse space or supply inventory. All I would have to do is bring in the accounts. It made a lot of sense for everyone involved. I made money, the plant made money and the client got their product. As I seized the opportunity, I wasn't concerned about how much the plant was making off of me supplying the accounts. I stay focused on what I make off each job. I don't care if they get rich off my accounts, because if it wasn't for them processing my jobs and doing the majority of the work I wouldn't make anything at all, in fact I wouldn't even have a business!

Looking back on my marketing company, some of the biggest financial blessings have been because I was not afraid to make other people money. To this day there are service providers that make thousands and thousands of dollars from my company. I could not imagine even operating my business without them. They are really the whole business, without them there is no business. That is why it is so important to take care of your employees, contractors and people who affect your overall business. Don't be scared to make people rich!

 ...some of the biggest financial blessings have been because I was not afraid to make other people money.

.e. People are naturally quick to jump on the agon if they think there is a little more to offer ugh someone or some place else. Many big deals .ıd great opportunities where lost for me because of the lack of consistency on other people's part.

 I think one big problem is a lot of people miss their blessing simply because they didn't hang in there long enough.

I firmly believe whatever you are trying to achieve in life in-order to be successful a key element is you have to be consistent. Make sure everything you do, you are consistent with your follow-up, follow-though and stick with it till you reach your goals! Don't always look to take short cuts or give up too soon because things didn't happen in a certain time. A lot of people want things to happen quick or in a short period of time and if it doesn't they're ready to bail out. Remember to stay consistent that's half the battle.

I can refer back to my internet business. I want it to generate consistent revenue, therefore I have to be consistent with it. We have an extensive marketing team that constantly solicits for new prospective clients and generates traffic to the website. We have a consistent advertising campaign that runs month after month on the various search engines to generate sales leads and traffic on the site. We also constantly refresh and update the website to illustrate growth and development with the business. Why would you want a potential client to come to your business a month or two later and nothing has changed, no growth, no expansion, nothing's changed. People love to be apart of something that's growing, a movement! It simply would be a turn off; there's nothing like a little extra motivation to close the deal. Even McDonald's has to come up with a new type of burger to keep customers coming. We are constantly distributing flyers to direct potential clients to our website and cross advertising and marketing with other companies. All this happens month after month; and sure enough the business is generating consistent revenues and showing above projected growth. This too can happen for your business if you just remember to stay consistent.

 People love to be apart of something that's growing, a movement!

How about consistency in your finances? I think this is a big issue for a lot of people. I know for years it has been my biggest argument with God. That's right I said it; argument with God. What, you've never gotten into an argument with God? If you haven't, I suggest trying it and see what God says and does. I'm going to share with you my personal experience in an argument I had with God over financial consistency. Unlike arguing with another person, God looks at your heart and your true desires not so much your personal frustrations as if you're in attack mode. You know; if you want to know how someone feels, what they really think and what they plan on doing, simply get into an argument with them. This is why I call it an argument with God. I needed answers and I was determined to get it.

One day I was down to my last few dollars and I had been struggling to find out if I was doing something wrong? I mean I had been working extra hours and putting my best foot forward, really working hard. But yet things still just didn't seem to be panning out economically. There where so many things happening around me and I just could not seize the opportunities. I was so frustrated. Although all my needs were met, I simply was just maintaining. I don't know about you but that drives me crazy; simply just maintaining. We are not supposed to just be maintaining! Let me repeat that; we are not supposed to just be maintaining. So why is that the case for most people? Through my frustration, I turned to the source; God. I told him I was tired of living the way I was and I'm working my tail off but yet I was not receiving consistency when it came to the finances. I demanded answers, what am I doing wrong I asked? He said,"You must learn to be consistent with me, and watch what I do." I didn't really understand what He meant. While being even more confused, I was determined and I wasn't going to let go until I had a clear definitive answer! I said, "What do you mean be consistent with you?" He said, "For example be consistent in your giving. Like in your financial giving in church you need to be consistent. Instead of giving various amounts in your offering, give the same amount consistently!" At the time I was stretched pretty thin financially, but I figured what in the world do I have to lose; I was going to try God, after all my plan wasn't working anyway.

 We are not supposed to just be maintaining!

So starting that next Sunday I began being obedient to what God's instructions were. My economic situation wasn't very good, so I decided to start with five dollars every week. As things got a little better for me I started giving ten dollars every week and than twenty-five dollars every week and than fifty-dollars every week. Over the years, as I became more consistent with Him, He became more consistent with me. It was just that simple! If you're experiencing consistency issues in your finances, you may want to start with your consistency with Him. This goes for finances, attendance in church, ministering to others and building His kingdom overall. Sometimes you have to try Him; as it is written in Malachi 3:10(NKJV) "Bring all the tithes into the storehouse, that there may be food in My house, and **try** Me now in this." says the Lord of hosts. "If I will not open *for you* the windows of heaven and pour out *for you* such a blessing that there will not be *room enough* to **receive** it."

CHAPTER 11

Appreciate What You Have

How does the saying go? You don't miss something till it's gone. I don't know about you, but for me I've learned to appreciate what I have even more over the years. I think as you get older in life you have a different kind of appreciation for things. I remember when I was younger, like a lot of people I didn't take care of the things I had. I wasn't very responsible with my credit. I didn't pay my bills on time and some I didn't even pay at all. Even with my first car, we called it Smilie, because when I got in a car accident I totaled the front end and it looked like it had a permanent smile on it. I wasn't very good at managing my money and overall my life was a complete mess. I can go on and on with the horror stories, but I'm sure you probably have some of your own. As I look back I realize how many things have changed in my life. How just going through life's obstacle course so much can take place. For example, I went from driving a beat up Geo Metro and renting an apartment, to driving a Mercedes Benz and owning a big house. It's not that I did anything special or I am any better than anyone else; I believe a lot of it had to do with simply learning to appreciate what I have.

I think when you learn to appreciate what God has given you to the fullest; He will give you even more. Over the years I have personally seen this manifestation applied in my life. Sometimes we take things for granted and don't really appreciate its true value. Or even better, sometimes we take people for granted and don't really appreciate their true value. If you haven't already found out, allow me to save you the trouble and the aggravation; the grass isn't greener on the other side! I've found the more responsible you are the more rewarding life can be. Some people simply choose to ignore responsibility, while others can't handle the responsibility. I understand at times things maybe tough but you've got to stay focused and try your best to remain consistent. Like with anything in life you get out of it, what you put into it.

 I've found the more responsible you are the more rewarding life can be.

No matter what it is you are trying to achieve in life, you need to look at where you are right now. Look at the things you have in your possession. Look at what God has blessed you with. Have you done right by your finances? Have you taken care of your car, your house, and your other possessions? What about the people around you? You have to ask yourself, do you appreciate what you have? I mean really appreciate it. Look at all that you have been blessed with. Sometimes we tend to go to God and ask Him to fix things or to give us things but yet we haven't done right by them... much less Him? I call it check yourself before He checks you. As it is written in Deuteronomy 6:18 (NKJV) it says "And you shall do what is right and good in the sight of the Lord, that it may be well with *you*, and that *you may go in and possess the good land* of which the Lord swore to your fathers."

So many times we are quick to move on from things and we haven't quite allowed its purpose to be fulfilled. What's the rush? Why are we so quick to walk away? You've got to learn to examine things from a different perspective. I try to step out of my own self from time to time and examine what's going on around me as well as the things I am doing. This is not often easy to do, mainly because we want to be right all the time and do what we want to do the way we want to do it, but by stepping back it allows you to have a deeper appreciation for things and a better understanding of the process you may have to go through to achieve it. It also may allow you to see what mistakes you have done and what you might need to do to fix them. Remember, whatever it is you have in your possession right now, if your desire is to have more, you may want to carefully examine how you appreciate it and what you can do to improve upon it. And through this new found perspective and self improvement, you'll see just how fast things can begin to change for you and your situation.

 So many times we are quick to move on from things and we haven't quite allowed its purpose to be fulfilled.

CHAPTER 12

Price of Opportunity

Understanding the price of opportunity can be one of your most valuable assets. For many, opportunity seems to simply pass them by, due to their own greed or lack of understanding. I define the price of opportunity as the loss one takes for not taking a chance or seizing an opportunity that is right in front of them. Over the years I have seen so many people lose precious ground in their pursuit of dreams simply because they don't take advantage of opportunity.

 For many, opportunity seems to simply pass them by, due to their own greed or lack of understanding.

Have you ever heard one-hundred percent of nothing is nothing? So many people would rather have nothing than ten percent, fifteen percent or even twenty. Greed plays a major factor in all of this. Many people feel because it's their idea, their product or whatever they deserve the bigger piece of the pie. I mean think about it, why should anybody put up all the money, take all the risk and make you rich? It just doesn't make any sense. Most people want others to take all the risk and they reap the rewards. Business just doesn't work that way. Once you understand the real price of opportunity, you will be surprised at how many doors will begin to fly open.

Sometimes you simply have to get your foot in the door. Just get some kind of break, that's all you need. If you were to talk to successful people, they will tell you it was just a shot in the beginning, a foot in the door, a crack that opened; anything and they took it and ran with it. I'm not saying settle for just anything, but sometimes *anything* is better than *nothing*. You have to decide for yourself. Super producer Teddy Riley said it the best. He knew when he got started in the music business he had to prove himself. He knew he took a deal that he wouldn't wish on his worst enemy. But he understood one thing, he believed in himself and his talent. He knew he would be very successful. See, I'm going to share with you probably one of the best things I could of learned in business. Everything's negotiable when you're making people money! See, Teddy understood this, he didn't sell out. He knew if he could just get his foot in the door; just get his music out there, prove himself even a little bit, he would be able to re-negotiate his contract. And now he's one of the highest paid producers in the business!

 I'm not saying settle for just anything, but sometimes *anything* is better than *nothing*.

I call it stepping out on faith. Sometimes you have to step out there, be bold in what you're trying to do. If you don't believe in it or yourself why should anyone else? This is a real big thing in the music business today. The industry wants you to prove to them you have what it takes. This could mean going out and selling your own music till you get a sufficient sales track record. It could mean garnering airplay on radio to prove that people outside of your immediate circle want to hear your music. The industry will actually accept someone who is less talented, but has their business together versus someone who is more talented and only has their talent to offer. I know it sounds crazy, but it's the reality we live in. It's all about having your ducks in a row. The more you can prove your idea or product the more the system backs you. It's that simple.

 Everything's negotiable when you're making people money!

How often does opportunity come knocking for you? In most cases it doesn't come very often, that's why it's so important to carefully examine each and every opportunity and the future it holds. Make sure you're not really passing anything up, even if it could be something small. Don't just look at the immediate gratification. Are you holding out for the wrong reasons? I've witness life changing deals get tossed in the wind simply because some people felt a better opportunity will come. You have to think what if that better opportunity *never* comes? Sometimes we are tested with little opportunities before bigger and better ones will come. If you are thinking about passing up an opportunity, you must stop and ask yourself am I prepared to wait for who knows how long before the next one comes? Can I handle the fact that I may never get another opportunity again? I don't know about you, but for me I have a hard time living with myself not knowing what could have happened. Not knowing if things could have actually worked out to my advantage at the end of the day, if I just would have taken the opportunity. I guess you can say it's all about how big of a risk taker you are?

 You have to think what if that better opportunity *never* comes?

As you evaluate the opportunities in your path, make sure you think about your overall goals and the role each and every opportunity can play in it. Don't let someone talk you out of your blessing. Don't let your pride or greed stand in the way. Don't be afraid to give up a lot to get your foot in the door. Believe in yourself and your capabilities; don't let anything stand in your way of success! Sometimes you have to sacrifice what seems to be a lot today for a greater tomorrow. Expand your faith and learn to take more risks. And most importantly trust God that he can turn even a wrong situation into something right. You just have to start walking, even if it's the wrong direction. What's it worth to you, are you willing to pay the price of opportunity?

CHAPTER 13

Everyone Is Connected

Have you ever heard of six degrees of separation? Six degrees of separation is the hypothesis that anyone on Earth can be connected to any other person on the planet through a chain of acquaintances with no more than five intermediaries. This is a very interesting theory. The theory that people are actually connected in one way or another through other people can be mind boggling. Notice it says connected, not related. I don't know if you believe in this theory or not, but it does make you wonder if it's true especially as you reflect on your life and the people you have encountered. I am a firm believer not just that everyone is connected, but that God allows people to come into our lives for a higher purpose, therefore creating the connection. I'm not going to try and convince you if you don't believe that, I'm simply going to share my perspective about it and my belief system hoping it will assist you as you continue to position yourself.

I am a firm believer not just that everyone is connected, but that God allows people to come into our lives for a higher purpose, therefore creating the connection.

For me, I've learned to be open minded when it comes to people in my path. I've noticed over the years I have managed to meet so many people from all different walks of life and various levels of financial status. I travel quite a bit; so I've been able to meet people from different parts of the country and see first hand how different the mentalities are based on their location. I've always believed there's a purpose for why we encounter the people we do. Whether big or small, I feel there is some type of purpose we just don't often realize it upfront. It's funny how God works sometimes. As I reflect back on my life; so many people that I've been connected with have actually turned out to be there for different reasons than I initially met them for. For a while I didn't think much about it, but as time went by I started to pay more attention to it. Often we don't pay much attention as to why people cross our paths. We don't really analyze why exactly we have encountered them in the first place or what is the purpose for our friendship, business relationship or association. That's just not something people do. As you think about the people around you, think about some of the conversations you may have had that stand out or what are some of the things they are connected with that interest you. Usually somewhere through those thoughts you'll find the purpose.

I've always believed there's a purpose for why we encounter the people we do.

One of the things I try to do is look for God, especially through people. As it is written in Luke 6:38, "Give, and it shall be given unto you; good measure, pressed down, and shaken together, and running over, shall **men** give into your bosom, for with the same measure that you use, it shall be measured back to you." God uses people to bless you. As I began to really understand this I started to look for God more through other people. I've realized God will use anyone, anywhere and at anytime to carry out His will and purpose for your life! Most of us tend to not recognize God through other people because we are looking at the person and not looking for God. As you walk through life trying to understand your purpose, fulfill your goals and strive for success, make sure you carefully examine those God has put in your path. Look closer at those people He has allowed into your life for there is a higher purpose for your connection, something better in store for you and for them.

I've realized God will use anyone, anywhere and at anytime to carry out His will and purpose for your life!

CHAPTER 14

Walk With Those Doing BIG Things

I've found if you truly want to be successful, you need to walk with those doing *big* things! I'm referring to anyone around you that's making things happen. You'll be surprised at how much you can learn from just simply walking along side them and watching or having conversations with people in general that are making things happen. For years this has been a strategy of mine in order to advance in certain areas and learn more. Why not learn from someone who is already successful and doing *big* things? Even if they are not in the same field you're interested in, you can learn so much about general business principles and ideas like never before. Sometimes all it takes is just talking to someone who knows a little more than you do about something to get the ideas flowing.

A lot of times we can acquire contacts and other valuable resource information just by conversation. Be sure to ask a lot of questions and listen closely to the answers you receive. I've notice many very successful people have a totally different mindset than the average person. Just about everything they do, they do differently and think about it differently. I once had a conversation with a very successful person and they where telling me about their electric bill. They said, "My electric bill during the summer time reaches as much as two-thousand dollars". I couldn't believe my ears! I said, "That's like a house note, a big house at that!" He replied, "Sure your right, but for me that's the price I pay for comfort, I'm use to it, I don't look at how much it is, I'm paying for the comfort." The thought process is totally different, if that was probably you or me, we would have passed out seeing a bill like that! Everything in life is based on perception, how one actually views things. If you think it's a lot, it's going to be a lot. In the music business, there is a big concept we drive. If it looks hot, it must be hot. The industry is about a lot of hype and inflated promotion. That's what tends to sell records. See, it's a business of selling people, if you can sell people you can sell anything. It doesn't always matter whether they can sing or not, rap or not or even play an instrument good. What it's about is how hot you can make them appear. If the public's perception is they are the next big thing, people react and support, it's just that simple! That's why some people buy some records and they may even listen to them for a while; and then when you ask them, why they bought it, they can't even tell you.

I found that people whom are successful love to talk about themselves, what they do and how they did it. This can be to your advantage, especially if you know how to listen and know the types of questions to ask. Many people don't have a problem even telling you how they did it because most of the time they feel you can't do it anyway. In some cases, they encourage you to try it for yourself and may even help you do it. No matter what they are talking about you have to appear interested, even if you're not. You have to ask the type of questions that will lead to opened ended answers and that will lead to other questions and then to other answers. What I mean by that is don't just ask the questions that you will get a simple cut and dry answer and the conversation is over. I tend to ask questions through what I call "theory" type methods. For example, I say things like, "I was thinking about doing this or that like this, what do you think?" Many times if the person has already experienced it or has ideas they will share it with you. I have used this method to get a lot of information, especially about things I knew absolutely nothing about.

 Sometimes all it takes is just talking to someone who knows a little more than you do about something to get the ideas flowing.

As you walk with those doing big things, you'll find that their success usually stems from big networks. You have to build your network, if you're going to build your net worth. It's just that simple. Networks are sometimes referred to as platforms. They can be very powerful if you know how to utilize them. Platforms can also be looked at in the form of mailing lists or marketing lists. There are two types of marketing lists; one you build yourself and the other is the one that others build. Most successful people utilize both types of lists to maximize their success. I call it cross promotion. Why would you want to just build your own list and only market to your base, when you can utilize others lists too and broaden your market base even further? It's much like sending out an email blast. If you only sent it to your address book, you have just limited yourself to your database, if you have others send it out to their address book too, you can maximize the exposure even more. This is why most people want to use the platforms of others. In music it is done in the form of having a featured artist on a particular song. If the artist that is featured has a fan base or lists already established, the new artist is now exposed to their audience. You want to build a large network in many forms. Whether it is an outside sales force, hundreds of thousands on a mailing lists or extension networks through other people, you want to build a platform that will be strong and effective that you will always be able to utilize when selling your products or services.

 You have to build your network, if you're going to build your net worth.

The more people you have around you doing big things the better. This plays an important roll in working on your mindset. I've noticed a big change in my thought process as I began to be around people that had more than I do and was doing more than I was. It's something about it that just drives you. It's hard to simply just sit around while others around you are making moves, having nice things and growing their businesses and careers. It's not about the mentality of not wanting them to have it. It's taking on the mentality that if they can do it, so can I. This sometimes can make all the difference in the world. There is nothing like peer motivation. The next time you have the chance to sit and talk or even walk with those doing *big* things, make sure you take advantage of the opportunity and seize it for all its worth!

CHAPTER 15

Favor

Some people call it luck, others call it blessing…. I call it favor. For many years I didn't understand what favor was all about. Like a lot of people I use to think things happened based on whether you did everything right or not. Understanding no one is perfect; I quickly realized that doing everything right has nothing to do with it at all. A lot of times we look at different people's lives and we say things to ourselves like, "What did they do that I can't do? I know more than they do. I'm more educated; I worked a lot longer than they have. I deserve it more. Why did they get the blessing and not me?" In the entertainment business this is almost a daily topic, whether it's a rapper or singer saying I can rap or sing better than they can, yet their song is on the radio and mine's not. Whether it's a manager looking for some type of deal for their artists and so many other artist less talented are getting all the breaks. How I see things, it all boils down to favor. Why do certain things happen in people lives and not others? The ultimate answer only God knows. A big part of this book, Position To Receive is designed to help assist you with your purpose and cause you to think about life and how you can open yourself up to favor from God. My pastor put it so eloquently when he said one Sunday, "Destiny is where you're going… Purpose is what it takes to get you there!" Are you focused on your destiny? Do you know what your purpose is? If you are not sure, don't you think its time you found out?

Favor I believe is tied into God's ultimate will for your life. I think as you keep walking through life and focus more and more on your purpose; God will reveal His will for you through the favor He gives you. I am a living testimony to this. I'm sure if you examine your life you will be able to find evidence of God's will, through favor you have received. A lot of times we just don't recognize it or acknowledge that it wouldn't have happened, if God's hands were not on us.

 I think as you keep walking through life and focus more and more on your purpose; God will reveal His will for you though the favor He gives you.

Passion and purpose I believe have a lot to do with the favor one receives. God knows the deep desires of our hearts. I think the question is more like, do we know what it is? Many times we find ourselves in things we have no business in. Some people get into different fields of work for the money or other reasons that simply have nothing to do with their purpose. You have to ask yourself, do you really have a deep passion for

it? I believe as we focus on the things w
passionate about, we also become a magn
towards it.

I strongly believe favor is when God moves people on
your behalf. It's very interesting when you think about
various things that people call blessing, how it usually
involves other people in one way, shape or form. There
is nothing like God making other people move on your
behalf. In my life, I can't even begin to give all the
testimonies of how God has given me favor by moving
other people. From how I got my house to my car to my
business to this very book you hold in your hand, it has
been nothing but the favor of God in my life moving
other people on my behalf. Without that taking place, it
simply would not be possible!

 **I strongly believe favor is when God
moves people on your behalf.**

A big part of receiving favor from God is learning to
trust Him. Trusting God a lot of times can be very
difficult. I recently attended a leadership conference at
my church when my pastor was speaking about this
very subject. He said, "There is a big difference
between having faith in God and trusting Him!" Many
people have faith, but they put their trust in other
things. They don't really trust God to provide or move
people on their behalf. Sometimes I've found in life

you just simply have to trust in God that He will work things out on your behalf. Especially when things seem like they aren't going to work out. We need to quit trying to figure everything out; we need to come to the realization we simply don't have all the answers! I think people put too much trust in themselves. We need to stop just believing in Him and start trusting Him for favor in any given situation. I believe as we learn to put more and more of our trust in Him, we will acquire a richness of favor in our lives beyond what we could ever imagine!

 A big part of receiving favor from God is learning to trust Him.

CHAPTER 16

Patience - In Due Season

Whether we want to admit it or not there is a time for everything. I'll be the first to say I want it to happen yesterday. Having patience can be a vital key to ones success. Being in the entertainment business has taught me a lot about patience. Like many people who work hard and look for the big pay off, you begin to realize it doesn't always happen or at least it doesn't happen immediately. I know this can be a hard pill to swallow for some, especially if you've sown years of hard work and dedication into something. Trust me I speak first hand. I've seen so many people lose their blessing behind simply not being patient. Most people jump at the first break and are willing to settle for just about anything; especially if they believe it will get them a step closer to their goals. Notice I said they *believe* it will get them a step closer, it doesn't always *guarantee* it will get them a step closer. This has always been confusing to me, but I do understand when your hungry and desperate you might just settle for anything. Is that always the best thing to do?

Once you begin to understand that nothing happens until its rightful season, only then will you be able to prepare your mind for the journey ahead. I've noticed so many people make a lot of careless mistakes because they want to rush the timing. As it is written in Ecclesiastes 3:1 "To everything there is a season, A time for every purpose under heaven:" Why do we want everything to happen immediately? Haven't you heard the saying good things come to those that wait?

 Once you begin to understand that nothing happens until its rightful season, only then will you be able to prepare your mind for the journey ahead.

I always tell my clients to be patient. Many of them want to do everything overnight. They're looking for that instant gratification because they feel they are ready. This happens especially when marketing new music. A lot of times this is the difference between an established record company and a newer independent record company. We tell them things like, "You want to *grow* there, not *go* there!" Most of the time it's not that we can't be successful, it's just we don't want to grow into the success. Sometimes in life this growth is essential. It is that inner preparation of our hearts and minds so we can fulfill our intended purpose. A lot of times it's not until that takes place the success actually comes.

Sometimes the best part of the ride is the journey. I mean think about it. Would we appreciate it, if we got it immediately? Would we have learned anything by just having it thrown in our lap? And most importantly depending on what it is, could we actually handle it?

I've learned that through being patient there is a big learning and development class. I remember for years I use to say I'm ready. Every year that goes by I would say I'm ready, I can handle this or I can handle that. I would also say things like, I've got the knowledge; I know what I'm doing. After about five to ten years of saying that year after year. I finally realized the truth, I wasn't ready. I wasn't ready at all. I think that's one of the toughest things to admit, especially when you want it so bad. Sometimes we have to come to the realization that it either just isn't meant for us or God needs more time to prepare us for what's actually in store. I'd like to think more about the later though and I'm sure you do too.

 Sometimes in life this growth is essential. It is that inner preparation of our hearts and minds so we can fulfill our intended purpose.

As you work to position yourself, remember to be patient as you pursue your dreams. Have fun along the way and learn as much as you can. Make sure you are really ready and can handle what lies ahead. Don't lie to yourself; if you're not ready, you are just not ready. Stay diligent in your pursuit; continue to work hard and be aggressive in your hunt. The pay off is right around the corner, the whole question becomes is it truly your season? Remember no matter what if it's for you, no one can take it away!

**"Therefore humble yourselves under the
mighty hand of God, that He may exalt
you in due time,"
– 1 Peter 5:6 (NKJV)**

CHAPTER 17

Focus – How Bad Do You Want It?

Have you ever wanted something so bad that it hurts? I believe we all have experienced this at least a few times in our lives. I can recall a business associate of mine always use to say, "By any means necessary!" His approach to life and business was always "guerrilla"; a take no prisoners type strategy. He said things like, "Shoot everything in site and let the paramedics sort it out!" Although I'm not that aggressive of a person, I do understand his approach especially when it comes to doing business. Sometimes when you want something so bad, you have to ask yourself; are you are willing to go the complete distance? Are you prepared to actually go above and beyond the call of duty to make things happen?

Focus I believe is one of the vital keys to achieving your goals. When you want something real bad, you have to stay focused. I'll be the first to say this is one of the hardest things to do in today's society. There are so many distractions to keep us from achieving our goals in life. Many people get caught up in either other people's problems or the many obstacles life throws at us. All this I believe is designed to keep us from staying focused. I can only speak for me, but I've learned that no matter what's going on around me in order to be successful, I have to stay focused. Sometimes this means working longer hours, prioritizing your life, learning when to say yes and when to say no and understanding how to work around issues; especially other people's issues.

 When you want something real bad, you have to stay focused.

Don't allow other people to drain you. This I think can be a very big problem when it comes to staying focus. In the entertainment business, this is a major part of our daily challenge. Everyone demands your attention, needs something done yesterday and loves to waste your time. We call it the business of the dreamer. In the entertainment business everyone wants to be a star, so they work overtime trying to get those around them to "dream" with them. They figure if they can get you caught up in their "dream" you will drop what you're doing and help make them successful. I've seen this happen too many times in my business and many people have allowed this to keep them back. I've learned after years of getting on other people's agenda, this has allowed me to put my own "dreams" aside and therefore ultimately holding my success back. Often this can be very difficult, especially when a part of living your "dream" may be lived through other people's success.

Everyone demands your attention, needs something done yesterday and loves to waste your time.

For example in artist management, as an artist manager you live your dreams as a manager through the artist. Unfortunately, you can't control other people's actions or how bad they actually want it. No matter how hard you work, how much time you put into it, or how much you believe in them; it makes no difference how much faith you have in them, your ultimate success is still dependent on the artist and their actions. This is what tends to lower your success rate when your dreams are lived through other people. You just can't control them. Over the years I have lost countless deals with the potential to be worth millions behind other people. I think ultimately that is what has allowed me to be even more focused driven and not allow others to stand in my way of success.

No matter what it is you are trying to accomplish in life, you must remain focused if you're going to be successful. I remember one day while sitting in bible study, my pastor began explaining the seven things you must understand in order to succeed in life. They were are as follows:

1) Life is not fair.
2) Life is never a problem and challenge free.
3) You can dress up life, it's still life!
4) Deal with everyday life or life will deal with you.
5) God never said He would help us escape.
6) Take dominion over yourself.
7) Learn to work under pressure.

I keep this list in my bible and refer to it from time to time to help keep me focused. I have chosen to share it with you in hopes it will help you also. Ultimately, no one can decide for you just how bad you want it, but one thing's for certain if you don't stay focused you may never get it.

CHAPTER 18

Layers Of Life

Did you know profiling is perfectly legal? At least the form of profiling I'm going to talk about in this chapter. We encounter profiling everyday; most of us just don't realize it. No matter what your race or background is we all encounter profiling. Whether you think it is right or not doesn't change the reality of the world we live in. What I am suggesting is that you recognize real quickly the layers of life society has us all in and learn to adapt. It's much like a chameleon adapts to its environment for survival. When you can't change your environment; the world around you, you simply have to make adjustments and adapt to it. Now more than ever it's about survival. If you're trying to get ahead in life and be successful you really have to learn to adapt.

 If you're trying to get ahead in life and be successful you really have to learn to adapt.

Understanding profiling and what I call the layers of life can be very important if you are going to be successful. Unfortunately, the world isn't very generous; we don't really own anything, as my partner and I say; we're just running around in it. For a lot of us we struggle getting ahead because we feel there is inequality. We have to work ten times harder than the next person to only receive half the reward, if that much at times. As we talked about before to be successful there is a certain type of mindset you have to have. I am going to share with you some of the things I have found out about profiling in my years of being in business. I hope they will either enlighten you or possibly make you aware of some things you may not know about or it may give you a different perspective about things you may already know about.

Unfortunately in business people profile each other constantly, whether it is a car salesman or a real estate agent profiling exists. People tend to look at things like what kind of car you drive when you pull up. If you're driving a high end luxury car must mean you have some money. They look at simple things like what kind of clothes you wear; shoes you have on or type of jewelry you have especially your watch. These examples are often used as profiling criteria. Although we don't like to admit it, the reality is what it is. I didn't understand it at first, but one day I decided to purchase a platinum Rolex watch. I notice people started to treat me different at places like banks, car dealerships and other places of business. Who would of thought a watch and some diamonds can make a difference? I'm not suggesting you go out and buy diamonds or a nice watch, but you must understand that in a society filled with profilers, you have to think about how to *position* yourself in your environment.

...in a society filled with profilers, you have to think about how to *position* yourself in your environment.

One of the easiest ways profiling is done is by subscriptions. Yes subscriptions, a lot of people don't realize the various types of publications you subscribe to can lead to other opportunities and information leads. Whether we like it or not, magazines, newspapers and other publications sell and market their subscriber list to other companies. I'm sure we all know what junk mail is. This often is how many other businesses get our information. For example, subscribing to publications like Wall Street Journal, USA Today, Forbes Magazine and other affluent business and professional publications can lead to financial related opportunities, whether it is credit card offers, investment opportunities or other valuable financial information. This can be very interesting, especially if you can get listed in the right databases! I know some people who subscribe to different publications not just for the magazines or newspapers themselves, but for the businesses they are in relationship with. Trust me, I'm one of them. I'm not trying to advise you to subscribe to all these different types of publications, but if you're trying to open some new doors in a particular field you may want to consider enhancing your subscriptions with field related publications.

Did you know there are layers when it comes to credit profiling? You probably won't find this in any other book, but it does exist. Creditors are able to purchase from various credit bureaus potential prospective customers predicated on a certain criteria. Not only can they sort lists by credit score (we'll go more into this in Chapter 20), they can offer lists by age, ethnicity, what city you live in, income level and really just about anything else you can possibly imagine a creditor would look to profile. Remember it's a business, so they are in business to provide information. The more they have, the more they can sell. I'm not sure about all the legal perimeters, but the way it appears, you can not tell a business who to market their products to. If banks want to market their products like credit cards or loans to the Asian, Russian or African-American community, they are free to do so. Understanding the reality of this type of profiling and layers of life can be to your great advantage. You must not focus on what you can't change, remember like the chameleon, adapt to your environment. This is why it is so important to understand the various layers and build a good profile with the credit bureaus and financial institutions (more on this in Chapter 20). Every bank account has a profile attached to it; next time you're at your bank make sure you check and see what your profile says.

 You must not focus on what you can't change, remember like the chameleon, adapt to your environment.

And last but not least, you want to look into joining various trade organizations, national associations and membership clubs in your fields of interest. This can be very resourceful for two reasons, not just because of the profiling but you will also be able to garner valuable

information about the trade and leads for va.
networking opportunities. No matter what the field
there are organizations, clubs or groups that specializ
in it and can assist you. The internet is a great way to
find leads for these organizations and groups. Although
it sometimes takes hours of research, it can be worth it
in the end. Simply search on your favorite search
engine for trade organizations or clubs that specialize in
your field of interest. You may stumble on to hundreds,
maybe even thousands of leads. Start researching them
and consider joining the ones you feel have the most to
offer, especially consider the national ones. These are
often stronger and have the most benefits. You'll be
surprise at what can happen and the types of leads you
can generate. For example, I joined the Independent
Book Publishers Association, better known as the PMA
as I was looking for help in putting this book out and I
also received all kinds of resourceful information. As a
matter of fact, the first thing they do is send you a
resource directory. This resource book is filled with
valuable contacts and publishing related information.
I've even started receiving different solicitations in the
mail for book related services. I found them on the
internet and it has already been a major blessing to me.

 **No matter what the field is there are
organizations, clubs or groups that
specialize in it and can assist you.**

Whether you have already established a good profile or
you are looking to start one, these are just a few ideas
and tips to keep in mind. Making sure you have a full
understanding of the type of profile you want to build

before you begin is always a wise decision. If you have already started to establish one, you need to investigate further into the details to find our exactly what it consists of, so you can continue to build and grow it to where you want to be.

CHAPTER 19

Opportunity Resources

How many times have you said, if I only had the money? Unfortunately the problem for most people is that they do not have what I call opportunity resources. With cost of living on the rise and the current state of the economy, it is becoming harder and harder to save money much less seize opportunities. For many of us, we have great ideas and investment opportunities that come our way, but we just don't have the resources to take advantage of them.

There are so many ways to obtain the capital one needs to start a new business venture, grow your existing business or even seize investment opportunities. Like most, I didn't have the resources when I started; so I had to start many of my businesses with little or no money. Mainly they were good ideas with a lot of hard work behind them. Although I have your less traditional type businesses, I understand you can't really get anywhere unless you have the much needed working capital.

We all know banks are in the business of lending money. Most of the time it's just not to those of us that have great ideas. I think one of the hardest things to do is get a bank to lend money for a new start-up business idea, especially if you don't have the credit or collateral (more on this in Chapter 20). It seems like no matter how good your business plan is or even your idea the answer seems to always be no. This can be very frustrating. I had one business person tell me don't even bother approaching a bank with a business plan, especially if you haven't already made money off the idea, it's a complete waste of time. Maybe you've already tried approaching your bank and have been turned down. What can one do that's in this position?

 I think one of the hardest things to do is get a bank to lend money for a new start-up business idea, especially if you don't have the credit or collateral.

Friends and family, I really don't need to say much here because many of times our friends and family are in the same position that we are in. Unless you're one of those people with a rich relative that just loves to help family members, this probably isn't too much of an option either. But no need to give up yet, there are some alternatives.

There are several alternative ideas you c obtain the opportunity resources you need. investors or venture capitalists. Often they can than your bank or normal financial institutions . are not traditional type lenders. Many of the gel investors and venture capitalists invest in ideas simply because of the management team in place, the idea or product itself or I've even seen some invest simply for a tax deduction. There are hundreds of angel investors and venture capitalists out there. Of course the internet is a great source to find some great leads. Simply put angel investors or venture capitalists in the search box of your favorite search engine and you'll see hundreds of listings come up. There are several companies that have a service where you can pay them to forward your business plan to potential investors. Some of them charge as little as fifty dollars up to a couple hundred dollars. That's a small price to pay to have your plan sent out to potentially hundreds of investors that are just looking to put their money behind something. Some of the sites even have categories like medical, entertainment, real estate, construction and more for potential investors that are interested in putting their money into a particular field. You might find a doctor or athlete that say they are looking to invest in a music related project or food service type business. It's really interesting how this service works, and a lot of them don't even charge a percentage for helping link you up with potential investors. One site comes to mind that has been used by some of my clients and they have garnered results is www.vfinance.com. I had one client that used Vfinance, to send out his business proposal. He was in search of $250,000 initially, once his business plan started to circulate in the business investment community, he started receiving all kinds of opportunities. One company liked his idea and plan so much they decided to revise it and send it out to their clientele base of investors pursuing even more money. They wanted to help him get one to five million instead. It would have cost him thousands simply to have the plan re-done. Also by soliciting his business plan he was able to meet some very influential people in the investment world. It even got to the point where he had one investor send him a contract on the spot and was willing to wire over the initial investment dollars upon execution. You never know what can happen when you utilize these types of services. However, they're many out there, so do your research and make sure you get good legal advice before entering into any agreements.

 There are several companies that have a service where you can pay them to forward your business plan to potential investors.

Corporate credit and personal credit are always available. In the next chapter, I'm going to talk more about the personal credit side of things. Corporate credit is a good way to go, if you have at least the resources to start a new corporation. Setting up a new corporation can be done real simple, quick and easy on

www.mycorporation.com. If you already have o.
would want to work on making sure you have a ‿
corporate profile with the various business cre‿
bureaus Dun & Bradstreet, Experian & Transunion
business solutions. There are several companies that
can help you establish company credit real quick, or I
should say quicker than going the normal route. One
that I've personally used and has been around for years
is www.creditco-op.com; they have a very unique
program at a low cost. There are several other
companies that will assist you in building a strong
company profile fast (details in next Chapter 20). You
can also start by setting up courier accounts like with
DHL, UPS, FedEx etc; a lot of these companies report
to the credit agencies. You can also obtain a corporate
Kinko's account and maybe even an Office Depot,
Staples or Office Max account if you have decent
personal credit to guarantee the business as you get it
off the ground. Other leads you can look into are office
supply companies like www.viking.com which is also
Office Depot and www.uline.com; they tend to extend
credit for a business without needing a personal
guarantee. Of course if you go these routes you will
have to use the services and pay the bills on time to
generate a payment history. It's just a matter of time at
that point. These are just some leads to help you get
your company credit established and start on your way
to building a strong profile, which will enable you to
get the business resources you need.

One of my personal millionaire friends told me about a way of raising resources that is perfectly legal and allows you to raise resources in the millions! It's called Regulation D offerings also known as Reg. D. I highly suggest you do your own research on the internet and consult with an attorney before attempting a Regulation D offering. There are different forms of Reg. D offerings; 504, 505, and 506. The main difference has to do with the amount of capital you are trying to raise. Raising capital up to a million, one to five million and five million plus dollars the choice is yours. Unlike trying to solicit for investors with just a business plan, Regulation D offerings will allow you to sell private securities. It is very similar to selling shares of your company like with the stock market, except you are doing it privately instead of publicly. There are even templates you can purchase and Regulation D start-up kits available on line for just a few hundred dollars. Most attorneys charge thousands to prepare Regulation D offerings. However, just like with business plans you can also have your Regulation D offering solicited through various companies that have investment pools and hundreds of potential investors waiting. Offering a Reg. D offering through these services usually garners even greater success of getting investors than just having a business plan.

In the next chapter I'm going to reveal ways you can establish your personal profile and obtain lines of credit at banks to further be able to capitalize on opportunities that may come your way. Sometimes in life it's about having opportunity resources in order to propel yourself to that next level of your blessing. Don't be afraid to step out and pursue your dreams, after all whom better to invest in than yourself. Opportunity resources are all around us, the real question is, are you willing to do what it takes to get it?

 Sometimes in life it's about having opportunity resources in order to propel yourself to that next level of your blessing.

CHAPTER 20

Building Credit, Eliminating Debt & Saving Money

There are so many ways someone can build their credit, eliminate debt and save money. In this chapter I'm going to share with you some techniques I have learned to help you with these areas. I'm also going to share with you several resource contacts and networks that you can further research to help you with additional information and strategies. They can also assist you even more with the overall process. Please be sure to consult an attorney, financial advisor or do a lot of research to make sure you have a full understanding before attempting any of these techniques. I'm in no way receiving a commission, own or work for or are a spokesperson for any of these companies. I am strictly choosing to share contacts with you and reveal some of my experiences. If you elect to use any of these resources, please do your own research and decide what is best for your situation. My goal is to share with you some leads and help you along in your walk.

I'm going to start with building personal credit. Many people already know about personal credit and who the major credit bureaus are. In case you don't know, the largest ones are Equifax, Experian and Transunion; and for those that may have never heard of the fourth largest, which is Innovis. If you haven't received your credit report within the last year, I suggest you obtain a copy from these agencies by contacting them directly; you may have to pay a small fee $8-$12 or go to www.annualcreditreport.com, where you should be able to get them for free. Once you get copies of your credit reports, you want to carefully examine them for inaccuracies and other information that may not be yours. If you do find any errors, you should contact the appropriate bureau to have it corrected. They will explain what you need to do. To obtain their contact information, either look on your report or look it up on their website.

 I'm in no way receiving a commission, own or work for or are a spokesperson for any of these companies.

Once you have completed that initial process, you are ready to begin building and establishing your credit further. There are so many ways and techniques that you can do to build your credit profile and score. Your FICO credit score is generated based upon information obtained in your credit file, scoring usually ranges from 300-850 and each credit bureau has a different score. The higher your score is the better, 750-850 being optimal. There is also a new credit scoring system started called the Vantage Score. One of the problems with the FICO scores is that each bureaus uses a different formula to calculate it, which means even if they have the same exact information their score will be different. The Vantage scoring systems is adapted by all three bureaus and will show a more consistent rating. The new scores, which range from 501-990, are associated with a letter grade from A to F (Nine hundred or above is A; letter grades drop every hundred-point intervals). This is just a another gauge, most likely if you have a good FICO score, you'll have a good Vantage and if you have a bad one, both will be bad. Some lenders such as mortgage companies tend to focus on your credit score. This usually gives them a gauge of your overall credit worthiness. Building an excellent credit score is very important in today's society; this by itself can give you the opportunity resources needed as we referenced in the last chapter. Although there are many ways, I'm going to share with you some of the most effective ways I've found to impact your credit profile and improve your score.

 Building an excellent credit score is very important in today's society; this by itself can give you the opportunity resources needed...

If you have bad accounts or negative accounts on any of your credit reports, this is hurting your score and affecting your ability to obtain loans and credit lines. Having these accounts removed or updated can dramatically affect your score. This is not often easy to do. There are hundreds of credit repair techniques and companies out there to assist you. You can either choose to do it yourself or hire someone to help you. I have found it is often faster and more effective if you retain the services of a reputable company. One I have personally used is called Credit Attorney, www.creditattorney.com; they have worked wonders for many people I know. There is a nominal fee to get started and an even smaller fee every month to retain their services. Depending on your situation, it can be well worth it! There are so many other credit repair companies out there, you can search the internet, but I must warn you to be careful like anything else there are a lot of people who promise or guarantee certain results and can't deliver. Also, don't just settle for the lowest cost either, learn what the going rates are and do your homework. If you like some people who would rather do it themselves, there are some great instruction manuals and tip sheets that really give you the tools you need to do it yourself. The manuals I highly recommend that are simply awesome are The Credit Secrets Bible! by Terry Price - Consumer Education Group www.creditsecretsbible.com, www.csbclient.com or www.truthaboutcreditrepair.com and Credit Mastery Guide Book by Traffic Network Central www.trafficnetworkcentral.com; these two resource guide books I promise will change the way you look at credit and the banking system forever! These guys are real experts in the credit game.

Turn your bad accounts into good accounts! Although this is not removing them from your file, it still can help give the illustration of a new payment history and help to re-establish your credit. This is basically contacting your creditors and working out a new payment schedule to build a current payment history. After doing this for at least six months to a year, it can begin to have a positive impact on your score. For optimal impact it's

best to re-establish and excellent payment histo
two years. If you can, the absolute fastest way i,
may also want to have these accounts settled ...u
removed all together from your file.

There are several companies that give you leads on
lenders that extend credit to those with bad or less than
good credit ratings. A lot of these companies charge a
fee for their list of lenders. Some provide detail lists of
banks and credit card companies as well as their
criteria. You can spend some time searching on the
internet for companies that provide lists; one company
I've found is www.youreapproved.org, they have a lot
of good leads. Sometimes, you may have to start over in
rebuilding your credit by getting a new credit card.
These banks work like second and third chance
financing for cars, a lot of them are willing to give you
another shot. This can help in rebuilding your credit and
establish a good payment history.

Probably the most powerful way to improve your credit
and score is to add aged accounts also known as piggy
backing. This is a technique that has been around for
years, mainly used by mortgage brokers to improve
clients' credit in a rapid amount of time. The easiest
way is to borrow someone's credit history. This is when
you have a relative or close friend add you to their
credit card as an authorized user and allows you to
share in their years of perfect credit history. Of course
they need to have a card with a relatively low balance,
preferably high credit limit and have at least a few years
of solid payment history. By adding you as an
authorized user, this usually means that the cards

payment history will report on YOUR credit bureau or credit bureaus depending on the creditor. You never have to even have the card, account number or anything. This is perfectly legal to do; it's just often harder to find a friend or family member willing to help you by sharing their years of good payment history with you. Some may even want to charge you for helping you. Speaking of charges, there are companies that charge you fees; and they seek out individuals that are willing to add you to their accounts. Of course this can become very expensive depending on the amount of the lines and how old the accounts are as these factors can have a great deal of impact on your credit score. So for those that may not have any friends or family to help them out or simply want to do it on their own and have the resources, there are several companies out there that do credit enhancement. I'm going to share with you one I've used before and it's called Seasoned Tradelines Inc. based in Florida www.seasonedtradelines.com; www.seasonedcredit.org; and www.agedcredit.com. There are several other companies, make sure you do your research. Be sure before you attempt to add aged credit accounts to your credit profile you have a clear plan of action, because this can be very costly and can be time consuming in working to have them removed. On the flip side, this can be of the greatest impact and can increase your credit profile and score by thirty to two hundred points without doing anything else!

 Probably the most powerful way to improve your credit and score is to add aged accounts also known as piggy backing.

And, lastly you would want to optimize all of the accounts on your credit profile. This means going in and making sure every detail of each account is updated, such as when your account was opened, payment history and current balance information etc. Scoring can be greatly effected by your debt-to-credit ratio, which means if you owe $800 on a $1000 credit card, your debt ratio is 80%, it's best to always keep your debt-to-credit ratio between 10%-25%. Of course the easiest way would be to pay your debt down. Like most people, that probably isn't the best option when you're trying to *position* yourself and you don't have the resources to just reduce your debt relatively quick. One approach you can consider taking as an alternative is trying the reverse way, instead focus on the credit and not the debt. This can be done by having new accounts like say a catalog credit lines, sub-prime merchandise cards or another easier line to obtain added to your file. What this does is change your debit-to-credit ratio. For example, by adding a $1000 credit line from a catalog company, if you already have say a $2000 credit card on your profile and you owe $1000 on it, where as your original debt-to-credit ratio was 50%, you now have a debt-to-credit ratio of 25%. This can make a big difference in your scoring. Sometimes it's even easier to change your credit side than your debt side or at least until you can pay your debt down. You may also want to balance your overall profile by creating a stronger picture. For example, someone with just a $10,000 line of credit is looked at differently than someone with a $10,000 line of credit and a mortgage, an automotive loan and a department store charge card. The latter paints a much stronger and diverse credit picture. So you may also want to diversify your profile depending on your overall goals.

 Sometimes it's even easier to change your credit side than your debt side or at least until you can pay your debt down.

While you're building credit you want to eliminate debt and save money. Some people's strategy is to pay off your smallest bill first by making extra payments and just pay the minimum on your other bills to keep a good payment history. Others try to consolidate their bills down and pay from there or start with the credit card with the highest interest rate. There are so many techniques to reducing your debt. One technique I found to be easy and allows you to do all three; eliminate debt, build credit and save money is taking out secured loans. What you do for example, instead of paying say a $1000 credit card off, you go get a secured loan against the $1000. The bank will put your $1000, in a savings account, and give you a secured loan and check against it. You than take the check and pay the credit card off you were going to pay anyway. Now you have a loan with the bank that you have to pay and probably at a much smaller interest rate than you where paying with the credit card. Now you continue to make payments over the next six months or longer. You have just eliminated the debt and this will build your credit up as they report to the credit bureaus. This will also build your creditability with the bank itself and you will be saving money at the same time because when the loan is paid off you still have your original $1000 in the bank. It's that simple! I call it forcing yourself to save money, and you clear your debt and build credit at the same time.

 I call it forcing yourself to save money, and you clear your debt and build credit at the same time.

Overall there are so many ways to build credit, eliminate debt and save money. Hopefully through these wonderful resources and a few techniques I have shared, you will be able to further *position* yourself to *receive* and improve your personal and professional life!

I will make you inhabited as in former times,
and **do better for you than at your beginnings**.
Ezekiel 36:11
NKJV

Message from the Author

I would like to personally thank you, the reader for taking the time to read my book and expose yourself to some of my beliefs, principles and philosophies. It is my sincere hope that you have been blessed by this book and that your life has been enlightened in some way. For this book you hold in your hand is just one testimony of God's favor in my life. I can't begin to explain all the favor I have received from the moment I decided to actually write it. I still don't know exactly what God's will and purpose is for it, but no matter what happens I'm going to exercise the principles I talk about in this book such as learn to listen, be consistent, appreciate what I have and wait for my season. Regardless of the outcome, I know that if I stay true and obedient to His Word, I'm already in **Position To Receive**.

Till Position To Receive Too!

ABOUT THE AUTHOR

Michael Matthews is a multi-talented music business executive, artist manager, business consultant, marketing guru, motivational speaker, option trader and author. He is the founder and CEO of MJM Management Company, Dominion Global Marketing, Dominion Global Publishing, Enterprise Records and Looking4airplay.com. He has taken digital delivery of music to radio and DJs around the world to another level. Mr. Matthews also speaks at music conferences across the country providing essential information to the industry. Dominion Marketing is currently one of the leading top retail marketing companies. He serves as a growth and financial consultant to businesses spanning many industries. Mr. Matthews has received numerous awards and acknowledgements for his outstanding business contributions and accomplishments.

 too!

Available Spring 2008

Other books coming from Michael Matthews

SELF MADE

Available Fall 2009

If you have been blessed by
Position To Receive,
we would like to hear from you.
Please send us your
comments & testimonies on how
Position To Receive has impacted your
life. Please only use your first name.

Position To Receive Feedback
c/o Dominion Global Publishing
P.O. Box 630372
Houston, Texas 77263 or email
info@positiontoreceive.com

**Selected comments & testimonies
will be chosen to be included in the
Position To Receive Too!
book due out Spring 2008.
First 100 submissions will receive a
FREE limited edition
Position To Receive Gift!**

Also available now
Position To Receive
CD Audio Book

Order your copy today
at www.positiontoreceive.com

For booking speaking engagements,
credit coaching, business consultation or
other inquiries:

Contact the Author

Michael Matthews
c/o Dominion Global Publishing
P.O. Box 630372
Houston, Texas 77263
281.277.6626

Website: www.positiontoreceive.com
E-mail: info@positiontoreceive.com

Recommended Reading & Listening

When Heaven Is Silent, Ed Montgomery
Breaking The Spirit Of Poverty, Ed Montgomery
Heaven In Your Heart-and in Your Pocket, Too!, Ed Montgomery
The Automatic Millionaire, David Bach
Rich Dad Poor Dad, Robert T. Kiyosaki
Understanding Your Potential, Myles Munroe
Boundaries, Henry Cloud/John Townsend
Healing – God's Medicine, Ed Montgomery
Prosperity – God Shall Supply, Ed Montgomery
Purpose – A Reason For Going, Ed Montgomery
Is It In You?, Ed Montgomery
"Show Me" from Day By Day, Yolanda Adams
Psalms, Hymns & Spiritual Songs, Donnie McClurkin
"Right There" from I Still Believe, Ed Montgomery Presents ALC
Mountain High Valley Low, Yolanda Adams
Position To Receive, Michael Matthews